ENGLISH FOR FURTHER EDUCATION

An O level language course
for individual and class study

CONSTANCE HAWKINS
Senior lecturer at Bedford College of Higher Education
in charge of 0 level English, GCE examiner

ROGER STRANGWICK
Head of English at Bedford College of Higher Education

This book is for people who are taking O level English Language or a similar examination in one year. It can be used as a class text or for private study. You will find sample examination papers at the end of the book, but it is very important to get some recent papers of the particular examination you will be taking. You should study them carefully and become familiar with the style of the paper. It is possible to get through O level English Language in one year but you will have to work steadily throughout the year.

Longman

LONGMAN GROUP LIMITED
Longman House
Burnt Mill, Harlow, Essex CM20 2JE, England
and Associated Companies throughout the World

First published 1984
Second impression 1985
ISBN 0 582 33148 X

Set in 11/13 pt Ehrhardt, Linotron 202

Produced by Longman Group (FE) Ltd
Printed in Hong Kong

CONTENTS

Unit two

Unit three

Unit four

Unit five

Unit six

Unit seven

1 Essays: planning

When essays are set they test you in several important skills:
1 thinking of ideas on a topic;
2 making them interesting;
3 arranging them in a sensible order;
4 dividing them into paragraphs;
5 writing in sentences.

How to start

Begin to plan your essay by trying to remember EVERYTHING you ever thought, heard or saw which has anything to do with the subject – then make a note of it.

1 Write your ideas in a list, so that you can read them easily, and leave space to add to them later.
2 Write the list on your answer paper. Then if you run out of time, you may be given some credit for points you *would* have dealt with.
3 If you think that the examiner will not be able to tell the difference between your notes and your essay, draw a neat, diagonal line through the notes.
4 Never write more than you have to about each idea: that wastes time and therefore marks. For example, write "Licence cost" *not* "People would think more carefully about buying a dog if they knew they would have to pay ten or twenty pounds a year to license it."

The place for complete sentences is the essay: the plan should be like a shopping list.

Making your ideas interesting

Compare these two lists of ideas written for the same essay.

My best friend

PLAN A		PLAN B
car salesman, Fords	doesn't smoke	Girl
age	has a Datsun	Name
hard up	loves garlic	Height
laughs a lot	lost plane tickets to Spain	Weight
local soccer team	quarrel over girl at 17	Age
drives too fast	stops his father smoking	Hair
two crashes	had motorbike, 3 crashes	Eyes
Birmingham accent	over 6 feet tall dark	School
met at school – 8/9	wants to emigrate single	Job
name		Family
going to Italy, June		

Plan A might take 4 or 5 minutes to write but an essay based on it would probably be lively, full of ideas and, therefore, interesting.

Plan B is dull – not because the girl is dull but because it includes no personal details which would make her seem like a real human being. The same list could become the basis for a really good essay – as *Plan C* shows.

My Best Friend

PLAN C		
Dull details	**Interesting**	**details**
Sex:	*Either*	*Or*
Female	not clear from a distance *always* wears jeans and a T-shirt (embarrassing example)	loves clothes, makes them, tried to teach me – failed
Name:		
Constance Beverley Entwhistle	old fashioned – hates it (e.g. of names she likes); initials = CBE!	known as J. (reason); views on real name and on married women changing names

Dull details		Interesting details
Height:		
5 ft 6 ins (1.67 metres)	taller than boyfriend, tries to look smaller (examples)	taller than husband, with high heels – doesn't care any more
Weight:		
Actual weight	*says* she hates being so thin but shows off (e.g. eats chocolate – makes me hate her!)	always dieting, thinks she's fat! 4 children = chips and chocolate, *she* eats yoghurt – strong minded!
Age:		
Actual age	17, looks 20 with eyeshadow (pubs, films), looks 14 without (half price on buses!)	40 – feels old, young ideas, usually tolerant (example), changed over years (example), me too
Hair:		
Colour	changes colour – e.g. green! Mother moans (ruins towels!)	brown, short – busy. Going grey, dyes it. Blonde at 17!
Eyes:		
Colour	wishes they were different e.g. thinks oriental eyes would suit her, make-up	short sighted, won't wear glasses – problems!
School:		
Name of school	behaviour at school and attitudes to teachers (example)	describe her *then* short, plump, naughty (example)
Job:		
Name of job	ambitious – aims to be supervisor in 6 months or marry boss (BUT *he's* fat, ugly, married. *She's* only worked there a week!)	firm, pay, boss, and parish council (traffic) runs youth club husband children hamsters

Plan C might take too much time in an examination – but if you can write this kind of list, you are already half way to writing the essay. Also it gives you very important practice in thinking of ideas *and* in sorting them out, so it is useful revision too when there is no time to write the complete essay.

■ *Exercise 1 Writing a list*

Write a list of everything you can think of about each of the following essay titles:

My Mother
My First Boyfriend (or Girlfriend)
A Man (or Woman) I'll Never Forget

Later you may want to combine several ideas in the same paragraph. Others may need two or three paragraphs each. Never worry about this: it is a sign that your ideas are developing well.

Thinking of enough ideas

If you find it hard to think of enough ideas, there are several things you can try.

1 *Choose a title you know a lot about.* (An "O" Level examination usually gives you at least six to choose from.)

CHOOSE	My Father	NOT	Benjamin Disraeli
CHOOSE	What It's Like to be Me	NOT	A Day in the Life of the Prime Minister
CHOOSE	My Favourite Pastimes	NOT	Fast Breeder Nuclear Reactors

2 *Make things up.* Unless an essay is about a factual topic – such as Unemployment or The Steel Industry – it does *not* have to tell the truth. So if the title is My Husband or My Father you can swap the real, live version for a millionaire with seven villas in the south of France, if it helps you write a livelier essay.

3 *Always include examples*. If the title is My Father, never just say
"He has a bad temper." Say:

WHEN he's likely to be in a bad temper;
WHY he gets annoyed by certain things;
HOW exactly, he behaves when he's angry;
WHAT you have done in the past to make him explode!

4 *Give several opinions* on what you are writing about, not just one.

My Worst Enemy

INTRODUCTION: Name, age, how long I've known him

MAIN OPINION:

Pompous – male	thinks he knows everything		
Loud voice	hear it across the canteen. Loud laugh – shows off		
Appearance –	scruffy: hair a mess, stands on end, too long; always same clothes (describe them)		
Other problems	stole my girlfriend last year (describe tactics) + good at physics, will get 3 'A' Levels. I shan't.	OR	thinks no woman can resist him, is popular at parties. Gorgeous wife. Ambitious – will get promotion. I shan't.

OPPOSITE VIEW:

Generous –	always lends things (examples)		always on time, often works late, up-to-date
Works hard	works in supermarket AND works at "A" Levels	OR	information AND runs scout group AND goes to night school
Tough –	broke up a fight, stopped trouble at Andy's	OR	didn't get Smith's job – didn't complain. Plays squash, painted his house.

CONCLUSION: still can't stand him!

5 If the title could have more than one meaning *think about the less obvious meaning FIRST*. For example, on My Place you may want to describe the house you live in but, in case you run out of steam too early, try writing FIRST about

> your place in society
> your "class"
> being "put in your place" by parents, teachers and policemen.

Write about your MAIN idea on the title last. Your other ideas are going to take only a few lines each. They will be useful as an introduction but they will be an anticlimax if they come after your main idea.

6 *Think again about how to include any ideas you could not fit in earlier.* Link each extra idea to the rest of the essay. One way is to *list* several left-over ideas in the last – or first – paragraph. For example:

Dogs

There are, of course, many things to consider about dogs: how much they cost – to buy and to keep; the dirt and noise they make; the exercise they need; their diseases; neighbours' cats. All in all, however, it is still clear that they may well be Man's (or Woman's) Best Friend.

■ *Exercise 2 Adding details*

Add *at least* one detail or example for each point listed below:

A	B	C
My Mother (or Daughter)	**Television**	**My Room**
age	4 channels	colour scheme
appearance	colour	money
habits	cost	size
worries	favourite programmes	furniture
job	portable	untidy
childhood	size	view
moods	censorship	defects
Dad	sport	virtues
luxuries	satellites	shared
feelings about me	detector vans	improvements

■ *Exercise 3 Listing ideas*

List your ideas on each of the following essays. Write main ideas on the left, with details and examples on the right for each general point.

a) My Hobbies   c) My School
b) Things I Hate   d) The Neighbours

Arranging your ideas

1 When you have listed about fifteen ideas on a topic, decide on the most sensible order in which to arrange them.

2 Next, number your points in the right order – and your list will have turned into an **essay plan**.

My House
9 house not big enough
4 near the church
3 in Northampton
13 new bathroom – best room now!
8 3 bedrooms
2 built 1926
7 garage
5 bells too loud Sundays (6.30 am)
1 parents' house really
10 2 brothers, share 1 room
15 Mum fusses – mess, carpets, Radio 1
12 eat in kitchen
16 polish smell Fridays
11 don't use dining room
6 garden too big
14 queue for telephone – bills
17 not perfect but I like it

A Man I Shall Never Forget
16 Christmas cards
5 super wife and 4 children
4 lecturer in physics
12 emigrated to Australia at 50!
15 spiders and wallabies
9 family in Hull
3 short, not thin
1 Bob
2 when we met
10 always repairing his car
6 homely, friendly
11 shooting – pheasant
14 bought land in Adelaide
8 never went anywhere new
7 loved parties
13 came home once
17 visit him?

3 Before you begin to write, you must have a clear plan of how to arrange your main points.

4 If you do think of extra ideas, add them to the list when you think of them. Never wait till you have finished the paragraph you are writing or you will forget them.

5 Tick off each point on your list as you finish writing about it.

■ *Exercise 4 Writing a plan*

Write a list of ideas about the house or flat you live in, then number your ideas in a sensible order.

Writing in paragraphs

Compare the following two versions of a simple story.

Version 1
The cat stretched thrusting out its long pink tongue and showing its needle sharp teeth the cat whose name was Percy suddenly sat up Percy had heard a noise a rustling and squeaking behind the skirting board Percy had also seen the tip of a whisker appear through the hole in that skirting board right next to the piano then without warning Percy sprang a mouse ran squeaking under the piano.

Version 2
    The cat stretched, thrusting out its long pink tongue and showing its needle sharp teeth.
    The cat, whose name was Percy, suddenly sat up. Percy had heard a noise, a rustling and squeaking behind the skirting board. Percy had also seen the tip of a whisker appear through the hole in that skirting board right next to the piano.
    Then, without warning, Percy sprang! A mouse ran, squeaking, under the piano.

Exactly the same words are used in both but the second version is easier to understand, because it is divided into paragraphs and also uses commas and full stops.

Usually it is very easy to sort your ideas into paragraphs.

1 *Use a simple order based on common sense.*
2 *Begin a new paragraph when you begin to write about a new, general idea* (not a detail or an example).
3 *Put similar ideas in the same paragraph* – or in paragraphs which are next to each other.
4 *Most paragraphs should be about ten to fifteen lines long,* so use about two paragraphs on each page and about five in an essay of roughly 500 words.

But any routine can become dull, *so make your essay more interesting by using one or two paragraphs which are obviously shorter* – perhaps for sudden changes in events or in attitudes.

Examples of paragraph order:

Early paragraphs	*Later paragraphs*
1 Obvious facts	*then* Less obvious facts
2 What things used to be like	*then* What things are like now
3 Points in favour	*then* Points against
4 What everyone else thinks	*then* What I think

For example, the list of ideas about A Man I Shall Never Forget, given on page 15, could be paragraphed as follows:

A Man I Shall Never Forget

Paragraph 1
(Meeting and *first* things I noticed)

1 Bob
2 when we met
3 short, not thin
4 lecturer in physics

Paragraph 2
(getting to know him – at home and with friends)

5 super wife and 4 children
6 homely, friendly
7 loved parties

Paragraph 3
(what he was really like – some faults?)

8 never went anywhere new
9 family in Hull
10 always repairing his car
11 shooting – pheasant

Paragraph 4

(sudden change)

12 emigrated to Australia at 50!
13 came home once
14 bought land in Adelaide
15 spiders and wallabies

Paragraph 5
(present situation)

16 Christmas cards
17 visit him?

■ *Exercise 5 Constructing paragraphs*

Choose THREE of the following titles. Make a complete plan for each one. Then write the first three paragraphs for each of them.

Travelling by Train (or Bus)   People I'd Like to Know
The Circus   Weekend Shopping
My Favourite Foods   The Tramp
Jobs I Hate   The Neighbours

■ *Exercise 6 Writing an essay*

Choose one of the titles you worked on in Exercise 5 and finish the essay. Aim at writing 450 words, using about five paragraphs, in one hour.

2 Language: writing in sentences

Writing in sentences is probably the most important skill that English examiners are looking for.

What is a sentence? It is a group of words:
    starting with a capital letter,
    ending with a full stop,
    with its own main verb,
    making complete sense to the reader.

Verbs

a) George **has** the ugliest face in Rotherham.
b) The girl in the bikini **is turning** red in the sun.
c) I **am** here **to read** the gas meter.
d) The television **has been struck** by lightning.
e) Samantha **will be riding** an elephant at the gymkhana.

In each of these five examples at least one word is in **bold** type: *the verb.* Verbs tell you what the subject of the sentence (George, the girl, I, etc.) is doing or, in the case of the television, what is being done to it.

■ *Exercise 7 Finding the verbs*

Underline the verb in the following groups of words. Remember a verb can be made up of more than one word.

a) You are going to be the proud father of twins, Mr Ramsbottom.
b) He will recover in a few minutes, nurse.
c) Tigers prowling among the cabbages.
d) My next-door neighbour has bought another fishing rod.
e) He and his wife having spent last summer holiday in Great Yarmouth.
f) You should complain at the Town Hall.

Making complete sense

In Exercise 7 there is something different about (c) and (e): they leave you needing more information, so they are *not* complete sentences. The problem is the verb. The other examples have a finite verb which makes complete sense; (c) and (e) have verbs – "prowling" and "having spent" – but they are non-finite verbs which are not complete.

Either the writer should have used finite verbs:

> Tigers **prowled** among the cabbages.
> He and his wife **spent** last summer holiday in Great Yarmouth.

OR Something should have been added. For example:

> Tigers, prowling among the cabbages, **made Uncle George give up gardening.**
> He and his wife, having spent last summer holiday in Great Yarmouth, **said they would never go there again.**

■ *Exercise 8 Non-finite verbs*

The following incomplete sentences all have non-finite verbs. Rewrite them so they make complete sense. Do this in two ways:
1 Assume that all the information is given.
2 Add something to complete the sentence.

a) Sanjeev, wandering along in a total dream
b) Being a couple of fools, Peter and David
c) Having beaten United, our team
d) Tomorrow being Tuesday
e) Grandma, being about to clean the grate out
f) To understand this difficult problem
g) Mr Thomas Hardcastle, being a man of few words and a councillor for thirty-three years

In speech incomplete sentences sometimes work very well, especially as answers to questions, so you could include them as conversation, between inverted commas. For example:

> "A crash! Ambulances – quick!"

■ *Exercise 9 Complete sentences*

Read the following piece and find the incomplete sentences. Then re-write the passage so that all the sentences are complete.

I am very pleased to provide the reference you want for Mr Kowalski. Although I have known him only six months. He is a man you get to know very quickly because of his friendly nature and approachable manner. Always laughing and making jokes in the factory or the canteen. He works hard as well and that is a rare quality nowadays. A man of humour and industry. Once he stayed on in the factory until midnight finishing an urgent order. I had to ask him. Because he was the best craftsman available. And the work being very complicated. Next day, he turned up as cheerful and busy as ever. And on time too. I would have liked to have made him a foreman. To give him the responsibility. Usually it takes a man five years on the shop floor to get that promotion. Mr Kowalski would have made it next month. If he had stayed here. Of course, I understand him trying to get on quickly. Having a large family and a sick wife. I could not give him the wages you are offering. Because we are a much smaller company and profit margins are low. I am sure you will find Mr Kowalski a real acquisition. All of us here are sorry to see him go. Really sorry.

Simple sentences

There are three kinds of sentences: **simple, compound** and **complex**. The basic one is called the "simple" sentence because it conveys one simple, *complete* idea. A "simple" sentence can be expanded.

For example:
"The cat sat on the mat"   could become
"The sable-black cat with the cruel emerald eyes lounged languorously on the blood-red carpet woven in old Turkestan."

The essential idea of the sentence is still "the cat sat on the mat".

■ *Exercise 10 Expanding simple sentences*

Using imagination and a few additional words, expand the
following simple sentences in the way shown above:

a) The ship sailed over the sea.
b) The man married the woman.
c) The girl bit the apple.
d) The wind blows the trees.
e) The dog lies in the kennel.
f) The insect settles on the flower.
g) Love was in his eyes.
h) The thief ran down the street.
i) Her hand gripped the gun.
j) The ring was made of gold.

Joining simple sentences

Simple sentences play a major part in writing but you need more
complex sentences for variety.

> The rain came suddenly. The streets were soon glistening. A few
> people had raincoats or umbrellas. Most were caught unpro-
> tected. They were quickly drenched. Drivers turned on their
> lights. The lights pierced the daytime darkness. The temperature
> had dropped sharply. People had been strolling in the August
> sun. Now they hurried along. A mid-summer day had been
> transformed into a winter evening.

There are too many simple sentences here, one after another. They
could be expanded but the passage would still read badly. Some
of the simple sentences need joining together to make the passage
more interesting. For example:

> The rain came suddenly and the streets were soon glistening.
> A few people had raincoats or umbrellas but most were caught
> unprotected and were quickly drenched. Drivers turned on their
> lights which pierced the daytime darkness. The temperature had
> dropped sharply and girls in flimsy dresses shivered. Men who
> had been strolling in the August sun, now hurried along. A mid-
> summer day had been transformed into a winter evening.

Notice, though, that the last "simple" sentence has been kept.
Simple sentences can often give an effective ending to a piece of
writing.

Compound sentences

One way to join two or more "simple" sentences is to use words like **because, although, and** or **but**. For example:

The rain came suddenly. The streets were soon glistening.
can be combined to make
The rain came suddenly *and* the streets were soon glistening.

This is called a **compound sentence**. The linking word shows that one action or event follows on from the statement in the first part of the sentence.

■ *Exercise 11 Making compound sentences*

Combine the following pairs of sentences using appropriate joining words:

a) The dress was a sombre shade of grey.
   The accompanying hat was shocking pink.
b) I must leave you.
   It makes me very unhappy to go.
c) He took ten wickets for the first time.
   The pitch was impossible for batsmen.
d) The wings are built in France.
   The tailplane is built in England.

Now try combining three sentences:
e) George ran for cover.
   It had started to rain.
   He still got wet.

Complex sentences

The other way of joining sentences is to use words like **who, when, where, which**.
Remember
1 The sentences to be joined must have a common element.
2 There must be a main statement, and an additional piece of information.
3 The additional information makes the sentence more interesting but is not essential to it.

For example:
  The boy caught the early bus. The boy was usually late.
Can be combined to make
  The boy, who was usually late, *caught the early bus*.

  Common element: *the boy*
  Main statement: *he caught the early bus*
  Additional information: *he was usually late*

This is called a **complex sentence**.

■ *Exercise 12 Making complex sentences*

Combine the following pairs of simple sentences in complex sentences:

a) I woke up at nine o'clock.
   The storm broke at nine o'clock.
b) I'll take the boots.
   I tried them on first.
c) Some of them were preparing to fly on to Greece.
   They will have a great holiday there.
d) The management gave way to the workers.
   They were demanding longer teabreaks.
e) Gianni's parents were at his bedside on Sunday.
   He died that day.

■ *Exercise 13 Combining simple sentences*

Re-write the passage below which is all in "simple" sentences. Combine them as "compound" or "complex" sentences or leave them alone as you think fit.
The Welsh Office have set up a working party. This group will prepare a "master plan" for the valley. The Welsh Office were very keen to take this initiative. Fortunately the local authority agreed. The Welsh Office believe the new Town and Country legislation fits the valley situation perfectly. That legislation provides for "action area maps". So far no "master plan" has emerged. Some local people believe it is taking too long. Those people are considered impatient by the authorities. A five-year time scale is in their minds. Meanwhile the "impatient" must be content with promises.

Sentence length

Short sentences

Use sentence lengths which suit the kind of writing you are doing. An average sentence length below twenty words will:
1 develop tension;
2 convey deep feeling;
3 be appropriate in business letters.

> It was fiendishly hot. Pacaltal sweltered in the implacable sun. The desert around the village reflected the light blindingly. Everyone was compressed by the crushing heat. Sweat was sucked swiftly into the arid air. Tempers rubbed raw. "There's gonna be trouble," said old Delgado. There was.

The atmosphere is created by a sequence of eight brief sentences. Re-write the piece in fewer but longer sentences. Is the effect reduced?

■ Exercise 14 Building tension

Write a sequence of short sentences describing the scene in and around a bank before an attempted robbery.

Long sentences

Long sentences can also be used to gain special effects, such as:
1 a lazy, relaxed atmosphere;
2 a feeling of pomposity.
For example:

> At the head of the parade, studded with local dignitaries, stalked the town crier, his dead tree of a body dignified by a livery of purple, yellow and lime-green chosen with impeccable lack of taste by the Lady Mayoress herself. Following this illuminated stick-insect of cartoon solemnity came the Mayor's coach dragged by two ill-matched and ageing nags who heartily disliked their Herculean labour of transporting the Mayor, a man of barrel-like dimensions, and the Mayoress who, though some six inches shorter than her husband, contrived to match him pound for pound in gravitational pull.

In these two very long sentences the writer is describing a scene which he thinks is ludicrously pompous. The long sentences help his purpose.

■ *Exercise 15 Slowing the pace*

Write a sequence of long sentences on ONE of the following topics:

a) A walk in the park on a dismal day
b) A fashionable and elaborate dress
c) A boring job

Varying sentence length

Contrast is very effective in writing and one way you can get it is by varying sentence length as in the following:

Brady controlled the ball deftly with one slight movement of the instep and then dallied arrogantly, foot on the ball, inviting the tackle. The fullback held off, nervously anticipating the change of pace which was clearly imminent. Brady drew back perceptibly from the ball, planting the possibility in the fullback's mind that control had been lost and underlined the possibility by straying his eyes towards goal. The bait was swallowed. A right foot lunged out. Brady moved with conscious speed. He slipped the tackle. A narrow path to goal opened. In the blink of an anguished eye, the ball was spinning in the net, Brady was jigging jubilation and the poor fullback sat contemplating the space so recently filled by the maestro.

In the first three long sentences the movement is slow because the match is static. *There are five short sentences* for the fast actions of tackling and racing towards goal. *Finally a long sentence* gathers three impressions together – the goal, the joy of one player and the sadness of an opponent.

■ *Exercise 16 Creating contrast*

Describe the following events, getting contrast by varying sentence length to fit varying moods:

a) A leisurely drive in the country where a sudden stop is needed to avoid a collision. Include the relief afterwards.
b) Observing two people meeting – one quick and lively, the other slow and deliberate.
c) Hurrying to get a train and relaxing in your seat after the rush.

3 Essays: descriptive essays

Changing your style

Your views on anything will be subjective – but that does not matter. Say what you want to say in a way which has an impact on the reader. But think about the style of what you write. Suppose you have to describe a room you know well. You could use at least three different tactics:
1 honest, factual description of the place;
2 the main facts, coloured by your opinions;
3 complete invention, right down to the magic carpet.
Compare the following introductions to the same essay topic.

My Bedroom

Version A (Factual description)

As you enter my room you see my single bed opposite you, situated sideways along the longest uninterrupted wall in the room. The bed has a pale blue bedspread, made of candlewick, with a pattern of white checks on it.

The wallpaper in my room is also pale blue, patterned with small white flowers: I chose the colour scheme myself and think it looks very nice.

On your left is the double window, which has pale blue curtains and which looks out on to the back garden. On the right a bookcase runs along the length of the wall, containing my favourite books, while above this hangs a painting of ships which was given to me for my last birthday.

The room is heated by a radiator which is situated beneath the window and my clothes are hung neatly, out of sight, in a fitted wardrobe to the left of the door.

Version B (Facts plus opinions)

My room is blue and white, private, quiet and tidy. The reason the white parts are still white and that it's tidy is that it was re-decorated last month and I haven't had time to ruin it yet. I chose the new wallpaper – blue, with a pattern of small white flowers – and my parents actually approved, so either my taste is improving or theirs is getting worse. The one thing we did disagree about was the carpet: it's white, plain white. My old one was mud coloured with white and orange splodges and it suited my lifestyle perfectly: there was no stain known to Man which that carpet couldn't hide. It was marvellous.

Mum, however, insisted. She said her daughter was old enough now to take care of things, that she was tired of wincing every time she opened my bedroom door and, anyway, I ought to have somewhere nice where I could take my girlfriends for a chat. I tried to talk sense into her but it was no good, so now I only dare to walk on it in bare feet. I even leave my slippers outside on the landing, leave alone my shoes – it's almost like being Japanese except I'd never dare have a tea ceremony in there. If I spilt anything on that carpet I think I'd commit hara-kiri – but not on the new carpet of course!

Version C (Complete invention)

A vision in blue and gold, my room is perfect. The blue damask of the walls has a soft, silken sheen, softly lit by the gold and crystal chandeliers which sparkle like the sun on a spring dawn.

Rich silken rugs caress my feet as I wander to the window to gaze at the gardens below. The vibrant colours of the orchids glimmer in the purple dusk and the perfume of the jasmine hangs heavy on the evening air. The song of a gondolier echoes across the water and ends with a sigh: I lift the crystal goblet from the table, the wine sparkles. Once more I gaze at my reflection in the glass – can all this really be mine?

Comments on descriptions A, B and C

Version A is probably truthful – and certainly dull. The writer's personality is out of sight. The result is a colourless piece of prose which shows no sophistication of ideas or words and is more like a map of the room than a lively essay. Notice the rather short paragraphs: these are often a sign that the writer hasn't been sufficiently interested in what he or she is writing to add entertaining details.

Version B is rather "chatty" – or colloquial – but the essay is written as a direct, lively "conversation" with the reader, and slang is realistic in the language of a teenager. The ideas are still clear because the words are clearly parcelled up in complete sentences and sensibly divided paragraphs. Most of all, this version is lively because the writer explains her feeling about the room. She even laughs at herself: for example, the old carpet sounded a bit of a mess, but she insists it "suited my lifestyle perfectly".

Version C uses a style that is rather rare in "O" Level essays. It is the appeal to the senses that makes this description different.

   Sight is used, of course: everyone who writes a descriptive essay realises that it is expected to say what things look like. This writer also uses the sense of *touch* (silken rugs), of *smell* (perfume of jasmine), of *hearing* (song of a gondolier) and almost of *taste*. It is a good idea to bring in as many of the senses as you can.

Describing places

When describing a place keep the following points in mind:

1 *Don't include every detail.* The reader wants to learn how it feels to be there, not how to draw a plan of the place.
2 *Do give your opinions.*
3 *Do try to describe it through all your five senses.*
4 *Do choose a place you know* if you have any choice in the matter: Most writers write best about what they know best.
5 *Use your imagination* and describe details which emphasize the character of a place.

■ *Exercise 17 Changing your style*

Choose ONE of the following titles and write about it in *three* different ways:

a) *one factual*, but unimaginative and rather dull
b) *one natural*, relaxed, personal version laughing at other people and/or yourself
c) *one rich, exotic* and appealing to the senses

The Party	A Garden in the Snow
The Procession	The Old House
The River Bank in Summer	My Car

Describing people

The advice on describing places applies to people too.

1 *You cannot describe a person properly simply by saying what the head and body look like*, you might as well be describing a corpse: you have to describe character, behaviour, relationship with other people, ideas – or lack of them.
Then you have described what the person is really like.

2 *Remember that general statements are usually dull, so include interesting details* – especially examples to make what you are describing come alive for the reader. Re-read the notes on pages 10–12 on Making your ideas interesting.

3 *As well as appearance, remember to describe sound, smell, touch and taste* if you can. For example:

He always sings operatic snippets when he's in the bath and you hear this through the wall;
he smells of sweet tobacco or of engine oil;
he always buys fish and chips on Saturday nights or smoked salmon on pay day.

4 *Think of people you really know* and take an interesting point from several of them to make up one special character.

5 *Do not describe anyone who is perfect*: someone young and sweet natured who never utters a cross word, for example. If you do, the chances are that your essay will be dull and disappointing.

■ *Exercise 18 Plan an essay*

Write an essay plan, and then the essay, on The Man Next Door. Read through your essay BEFORE you give it in for marking. Does the man seem real? If not, try again: include bad points as well as good ones. Say where he works, how well he drives his car, whether he kicks the cat when he's angry.

4 Words: how to say it

Mood and style

Decide on a mood which suits the purpose of your writing – for example, business-like, casual, romantic or ghostly – then search for words which fit that mood.

Clichés

A cliché (pronounced clee–shay) is a group of words which has been used so often that people could finish your sentence for you when you have hardly begun it. For example:

It's lovely weather for the time of year.
I've never been so insulted in all my life.
I don't know what the world's coming to.
I blame the parents myself.
I nearly died!

Ideas which are predictable usually mean a weak, boring, even a bad essay. Words and groups of words which are predictable are also monotonous – so do not use clichés.

Negatives and apostrophes

can't
don't
didn't
shan't
haven't
couldn't
shouldn't

The apostrophe is always near the end, between the -n and the -t *every* time, to show the letter o is missing.

If other letters are missing too, forget about them – you use only one apostrophe per word. For example -ll gets lost when "shall not" changes to "shan't", but the apostrophe still crops up before the final -t and nowhere else.

Double negatives

Two negative words in the same statement about the same subject cancel each other out. For example:
The man who said "I *don't* want *none* of your cheek", probably meant that he didn't want *any* of it, but in fact he said that he wanted some.
He *should* have said:
Either "I *don't* want ANY of your cheek!"
Or "I *want* NONE of your cheek!"
You *can* use the word "No" itself as well as another negative word, when "No" is used as the opposite of "Yes", then followed by a *separate* explanation.

> No, *I don't* want a pay rise thank you.
> No, it's *not* raining in Manchester today.
> No, I *haven't* been to Outer Mongolia.

Each of these sentences is still negative, because the word "No", in each one, is simply a separate confirmation of what follows it.

■ *Exercise 19 Style*

Describe briefly the mood and language which would suit each of the following descriptions of the *same* burglary:

a) a policewoman's report
b) a local newspaper report
c) the houseowner's description, in a letter to a friend
d) the story of the householder's ten year old son, at school the next day.

Write two accounts, showing two different styles of writing. Each version should be about 200 words long and include the same basic situation and events.

■ *Exercise 20 Clichés*

Underline all the clichés in the following extract. Then re-write the passage, avoiding all dull, predictable language but keeping the same situation.

I looked anxiously at the clock: he was late – it was midnight and I was worried to death. What could I do? If I rang the police and then he just turned up on the doorstep I'd feel such a fool.

I knew I had to pull myself together, so I put the kettle on and made myself a cup of strong black coffee to calm my nerves. Suddenly the doorbell rang and somehow I knew that something dreadful had happened. I opened the door. "Mrs Smith? I'm Constable Jones. I'm afraid there has been an accident . . ."

I can't remember anything about the next few hours, it was all like a nightmare – I just couldn't believe that it was happening to me. Everybody was very kind, of course: they did what they could to help and everyone said that Time was a great Healer. My neighbours were marvellous – they couldn't do enough for me. But Rover, run over by a bus! Tears kept on rolling down my cheeks. No other dog would ever be the same.

■ *Exercise 21 Negatives*

Write seven negative sentences, one for each of the negative words listed on page 31, making sure you get the apostrophe in the right place – and that you have said "No" when you think you have.

■ *Exercise 22 Double negatives*

Each of the following sentences is trying to say "No". Removing the unnecessary word(s), re-write the sentences so that each one really is negative.

a) You can't bring no dogs into this cake shop.
b) Jean said, "No! You didn't tell him that you don't want none?"
c) I shan't stay here no longer! Not if you're going to behave like this!
d) I'll never tell no more lies for you!

5 Spelling: words ending in -l

fill ⎫
till ⎬ use -ll
full ⎭

(full + fill) = fulfil ⎫
⎬ Use one -l at a time
(un + till) = until ⎭

awe + full = awful
beauty + full = beautiful
care + full = careful
dread + full = dreadful
fear + full = fearful
harm + full = harmful

Look carefully at words which end in -ful, and DO NOT see double. Remember the instruction "fill till full" and that each of these three words loses an -l when other letters are joined on in front.

6 Exercises for revision

■ *Exercise 23 Ideas*

Choose THREE of the following essay titles and list your ideas on each one. Use two columns, one for general points, the other for interesting details.

What It's Like to be Me	The Rubbish Dump
The Canteen	Dreams
The Bus Station on a Busy Day	The Motorbike
Our Indoor Shopping Centre	My Village or Town
A Normal Day at College/Work/School	Strangers I Know by Sight

■ *Exercise 24 Planning*

a) Number each point you have listed in Exercise 23, in the order you would use when writing the essays. Then re-write the lists using the new order.

b) Indicate, in the margin, which points should be grouped together in each paragraph (see the example on page 17).

■ *Exercise 25 Essays*

Write one of the essays you have now planned and aim at writing 450 words. Give yourself an hour to do this.

■ *Exercise 26 Finite verbs*

In the following passage there are a number of gaps. Fill them using the appropriate form of the suggested verb. (In the first gap you could write "breaks".)

If that washing machine _____ (to break) down once more, I _____ (to go) to send it back. We _____ (to have) it two weeks and it _____ (to break) down five times already. You _____ (to persuade) me to buy an automatic although I really _____ (to want) a twin-tub. On Tuesday there _____ (to be) water all over the kitchen and heaven _____ (to know) what _____ (to happen) tomorrow when I _____ (to wash) these blankets. Probably it _____ (to explode).

■ *Exercise 27 Sentence construction*

Find the incomplete sentences in the following passage and then re-write it so that all of the sentences are complete.

As the day of the championship approaches. That makes the tension increase. All the people associated with the fighter snap at each other and get really mean. A bit like dogs in a crowded cage. The fighter himself is in tip-top shape and he gets really on edge. Any little thing out of place nettles him. He would thump his best friend. Even his wife. I saw that happen once. She was just having a little joke but the chap could not take it. Tears everywhere afterwards. He was so furious he wanted to smash somebody else to prove it was somebody else's fault. Like the manager. Or the trainer. Of course, they turned it all on the opponent. To make him even more aggressive. Anyway the fellow won the fight and his wife got a diamond necklace worth a cool two thousand. Probably worth a black eye. She was lucky though. Him being only a featherweight.

■ *Exercise 28 Sentence constuction*

Write a sequence of twelve "simple" sentences on one of these topics. Then re-write the sequence, combining the simple sentences into compound or complex sentences where you think it is helpful.

a) The sky on a clear, dark night
b) A supermarket
c) An old tramp on the road
d) A hospital ward
e) A motorway

■ *Exercise 29 Building tension*

Write a description of one of the following using mostly short sentences to give the atmosphere. Use about 100 words.

a) An exciting point in a car race with one car trying to overtake another for the lead.
b) An unpleasant dream in which you are being chased.
c) The scene at a fire.

■ Exercise 30 Fitting the mood

Write a description of one of the following in three long sentences:

a) A crocodile basking beside a slow, muddy river in tropical heat
b) A slow greedy eater deliberately demolishing a meal
c) Someone doing embroidery with careful skill

■ Exercise 31 Changing your style

The following passage is badly written. Re-write the passage in more suitable language. Do not change the basic facts.

Jayne (16-year-old daughter): Mother, I wonder whether I might request a favour.
Mother: I am rather preoccupied at the moment: a pipe has burst in the bathroom and I didn't discover it until the dining room ceiling collapsed beneath the weight of the leaking water.
Jayne: How unfortunate! May I help you repair the damage?
Mother: I'm grateful for your consideration. Perhaps you could call your father in from the garden and request his help in turning off the water supply. Meanwhile I shall telephone for the plumber and remove the debris from the dining room.
Jayne: Of course Mother, and I can easily postpone my evening appointment with George and help you to clear away the mess.

■ Exercise 32 Essays

Using a picture from a newspaper or magazine write *first* the essay plan, *then* an essay, on one of the characters.

■ Exercise 33 Clichés and negatives

Some of these sentences contain clichés *and* double negatives. Re-write them so the meaning is clear. Replace the clichés with your own words.

a) I don't know how he does it on his pension: he's never had no extra help and he always looks so spick and span.
b) "Don't tell me you call yourself a painter and decorator. You're no more a skilled workman than I'm the Emperor of China. Rub that down and have another go – and don't give me no excuses."

c) It's a shame my blue dress is still at the cleaners – "Industrial dispute," the girl said – she was ever so nice about it though, you could tell she was really sorry. "All the same these delivery men," she said, "no sense of responsibility, they just don't care, never mind the customers, oh no!"

d) I never thought you'd leave me to see to it all on my own: you could have had a bit more consideration but you've never shown no respect for my feelings since you began going round with that crowd of young hooligans!

e) "It's the happiest day of your life," they all said. Of course it's easy for them to talk, they don't know the half of it.

f) It's all very well bringing a fine bouncing baby into this world but it's a hard life bringing up children these days. Those know-alls don't know nothing yet – just wait till they've got four little treasures each, like me.

■ *Exercise 34 Spelling and apostrophes*

Correct the spelling in the following passage and make sure apostrophes are in the right place.

"Dreadful!" she said, "I new we were in for a bad time but I didn't think it would be quiet as awfull as this."

"What can I do?" I answered. "We have'nt had a holiday for five years, I need a new coat and hear we are with a gas bill for over ninety pounds! We just cant pay it. We'll have to ask for time to pay – perhaps they'l let us pay monthly til its all paid off."

"But it's humiliating," she said, her eyes ful of tears. "I've never been in debt before. Its shamefull the way your firm sacked you with only a week's notice, dont they now how hard it is for a man to find work these days?"

■ *Exercise 35 Spelling*

Re-read the list of words which end in -ful, given on page 34. Find another ten words which end in -ful and use each one in a complete sentence.

UNIT TWO

1 Comprehension: factual passages

A piece of factual writing sets out an argument or a description or gives an idea or opinion. A comprehension exercise based on a factual passage will ask questions to test your understanding of the passage and the intention of the writer.

Types of question

Certain types of question turn up regularly:

1 *Questions which ask you to pick out facts.*
   These are the easiest questions. If you have read the passage with care, you should have no problems.
2 *Questions which ask you the meaning of a word or phrase.*
   You must give the meaning used in the passage.
3 *Questions which ask you to gather information.*
   The passage might give details of a person's character in different places and you might have to blend these into a full description.
4 *Questions which ask you to comment on what has been written.*
   You have to justify your comments by reference to the passage. You can disagree with the writer but you must give sound reasons for disagreeing.

Of course, you may have a question that does not fit into one of the categories given. It is important to get a lot of practice in answering comprehension questions. This will give you confidence.

Tackling a comprehension exercise

There are three *main* steps in tackling a comprehension exercise. If you follow them every time, you will not throw marks away.

1 *Read the passage carefully.*
   This is the *first* step. Do not read the questions first because then you will be looking for answers and you will not read properly. It is vital to read thoroughly. Taking notes or stopping after each

paragraph to think about what you have read can help. Some parts may be hard to understand. Do not give up. Try to work out the meaning. If it is a practice exercise, use any dictionary or reference book to help you. Of course, in the examination books will probably not be allowed.

2 *Read the question carefully.*
Every year people fail examinations because they do not read the questions properly. Do not start an answer, until you are *sure* what the question means.

3 *Answer the questions carefully.*
This is the *final* stage. You will probably have to make notes from the passage and produce a rough answer. You can change this until you are satisfied and then write the neat version.

Qualities of a good answer

A good answer will:
1 *Be written in complete sentences* unless it is clear that sentences are not needed. Remember, too, an answer can be more than one sentence.
2 *Use different words from the original passage.* You will not be able to change every word but as much variety as possible will show you have a good knowledge of words and their meanings.
3 *Use only the material in the passage.* You may know a lot more about the subject but you must base your answers only on what you have read.
4 *Answer the question.* Even if you write well, you will not get a good mark unless you answer the question that was set. Check that you have.

Model comprehension exercise

Here is a comprehension exercise. Read the passage and then study the questions, comments and suggested answers that follow it:

In the autumn of my seventeenth year, I decided to write a novel. I went off one evening and bought myself the thickest quarto writing pad, in pale blue, that I could find. I bore home that massive chunk of writing paper with a feeling of rare and
5   peculiar excitement in my heart: an emotion arising from a

particular sort of anticipation that has since been repeated a
thousand times. Talking only the other day to a celebrated
painter, I discovered that she too had shared over and over again,
the same anticipatory thrill: hers from a blank area of canvas,
10 mine from a naked quarto of paper. What, eventually, is going
to illuminate the canvas, what the paper? The question is still,
for me, the most exciting one of a writer's life – out of, and by
means of, the simplest materials, will come what? Almost every
morning that autumn and winter, I settled down to write.
15 Progress was mostly undisturbed, peaceful and rapid. I wrote
like a hermit. This is not to say that I cut myself off completely
from the world of football, from the cinema, or, when summer
came round again, from cricket, tennis and much bicycling into
the countryside. That hermit-like part of my existence was merely
20 a first demonstration of the indisputable fact that creation in art
of any kind is, of necessity, secret. The fusion between writer
and paper, painter and canvas, cannot, or should not, be shared.
It is beyond all dispute that my hermit-like industry did not
prevent my novel from being an untidy, verbose and appalling
25 shambles. When it was finished, I sent it off to Edmund Kirby,
who in reply permitted himself a few comments of such a
guarded nature that I was disposed to submit to the verdict that
I had spawned a shapeless, amateurish, useless monster. Indeed
I had. A certain buoyancy of character is something I have never
30 lacked and with very little protracted pain I buried the blue
bundle of words away in a drawer like a creature still-born. But
the world being full of novels that are begun but never finished,
I had at least this singular piece of satisfaction to comfort me:
bad as it might be, I had finished.

H E Bates

Questions

1 *What pastimes did the author enjoy apart from writing his novel?*
This question tests your reading of the passage. Careful reading
will tell you that the information required is in lines 16–19. The
suggested answer is:
   He enjoyed playing football and going to the cinema. In
   summer he liked cricket and tennis and long cycle-rides in
   the country.

2 *Choose four of the following words. For each of the words chosen, give
a word or phrase that could be used to replace it in the passage.*
   celebrated (line 7)
   rapid (line 15)
   demonstration (line 20)
   indisputable (line 20)
   spawned (line 28)
   protracted (line 30)

This tests your knowledge of words and their meanings. Notice
the word or phrase you give should be able to *replace* the word
given. If it could not *replace* the word, you will lose marks even
if the meaning is correct.

Here are the suggested answers. Check that each fits into the
passage:

celebrated (line 7)	**famous**
rapid (line 15)	**quick**
demonstration (line 20)	**indication**
indisputable (line 20)	**unquestionable**
spawned (line 28)	**given birth to**
protracted (line 30)	**drawn-out**

3 *Give in your own words the meaning of*
   permitted himself a few comments of such a guarded nature (lines
   26–27)
   a certain buoyancy of character is something I have never lacked
   (lines 29–30)

These two quite hard extracts test your understanding again.
Putting them into *your own words* shows you grasp the meaning.
The suggested answers are:

   allowed himself to make one or two cautious points
   I have always been able to bounce back after a setback

A dictionary can be very helpful for questions like 2 and 3. You
might find a thesaurus useful, too.

4 *What factual details about the novel do you learn from the passage?*
This question asks you to collect information and decide

whether it is factual or not. In lines 2–3 you are told that the book was written on "pale blue" paper of "quarto" size. These are factual details. Later, the author calls his novel "an untidy, verbose and appalling shambles" and "a shapeless, amateurish, useless monster". These are forceful views but they are *opinions* not facts. You learn only one more fact: the novel was finished. The suggested answer is:

> The novel was finished. It was handwritten on pale blue quarto paper.

5 *What words in the passage show the writer's criticism of his work?*
The two opinions discarded in question 4 are useful here. They show the writer's dissatisfaction with his efforts. The suggested answer is:

> The two descriptions of the novel as "an untidy, verbose and appalling shambles" and "a shapeless, amateurish, useless monster" indicate the writer's view of his efforts.

6 *Explain in your own words what a writer has in common with an artist.*
This requires you to search, gather and translate. The information needed is in lines 7–13. It needs to be summarised in your own words. The suggested answer is:

> They share a sense of expectancy. Each has a clean surface to be filled. The exciting question is what will be the outcome of their efforts.

7 *What did the boy learn from writing "like a hermit"?* (lines 15–16)
The answer is not in line 15–16. The key is in the sentence where the word "hermit" (line 19) is used again. That sentence states that writing "cannot, or should not, be shared". The suggested answer is:

> He learnt that the act of producing a work of art is essentially a private activity.

8 *What feelings were experienced by the boy in writing his novel?*
This almost demands a summary of the whole passage. At first, there is the "anticipatory thrill", in the second paragraph the boy savours the private pleasure of writing and at the end he realises that the novel is bad but retains a sense of achievement at having completed it. The suggested answer plots this development.

At first, he felt excited at the prospect of writing. Gradually he sensed the private nature of the activity. When it was over, he was proud of his achievement but still realised that his first novel was a failure.

Exercise 1 A comprehension piece

Read the following passage and answer the questions in sentences:

Transfusions

Blood transfusions were an idea of Christopher Wren. In 1665, he suggested to a Dr Lower that blood might be passed from one animal to another. The transfusion worked. Two years later, Mr Arthur Cogan passed blood into himself from a pig with, it is claimed, no ill-effects. In France one of Louise XIV's doctors gave a patient a transfusion of lamb's blood and, despite a violent reaction, the patient lived. In 1668 an unfaithful husband was given calf's blood in the hope he would take on the placid character of the animal. The husband died.

After that catastrophe, transfusions were banned in France. In 1818 Dr J Blundell of London attempted a transfusion of human blood. The patient died. One trouble was the clotting of the blood and many ideas were tried to keep the blood fluid. Success was soon achieved but transfusion was still hazardous. Some transfusions succeeded; others were disastrous. Not until 1901, did Landsteiner solve the riddle of blood groups.

Now transfusions are common. Over 2,000,000 Americans have them every year and Britain uses over a million bottles of blood and plasma annually. There are banks of extremely rare blood, as at the Chelsea Naval Station, Massachusetts (where, for example, Rh-null is kept, reported so far in only five people). Jehovah's Witnesses, however, are against transfusions. They will accept treatment but not blood and quote the Bible as authority. There are 52,000 active Witnesses in Britain, twice the number ten years ago, and they get huge publicity when lack of transfusion precedes a death. Mr Walter Stevens, for example, refused permission in June 1965 for his wife to receive blood during a difficult delivery. She died shortly after, and the press were quick to pounce.

The Body A Smith (adapted)

Questions

1 What sort of blood was the 1668 patient given?

2 Why was this sort of blood given?

3 Give an example of the rare bloods kept at the Chelsea Naval Station.

4 What problem did Landsteiner solve?

5 What authority do Jehovah's Witnesses quote against transfusion?

6 Name three animals used as donors in the early days of transfusion?

7 What was Christopher Wren's contribution to blood transfusion?

8 How many Jehovah's Witnesses were there in Britain ten years before this piece was written?

9 How much blood and plasma is used annually in Britain for transfusion?

10 Which problem was solved first – that of blood groups or that of clotting?

■ Exercise 2 Meanings of words and phrases

Read this passage and answer the questions. If you have difficulties, work out a meaning by careful reading. As a *last* resort, use a dictionary.

What has the future in store? Is it going to get noisier? What new techniques will there be to control noise?

Quiet costs money. No manufacturer of engines is going to pursue quietness simply for philanthropic reasons. Even now the
5 strides made in the design of quieter turbo-fan engines are not automatically of benefit to us. Give an airline quieter planes, and the pilots will employ more power after take-off and still keep within the limits of airport noise regulations. A machine manufacturer will endeavour to make a quieter product only if
10 he is compelled to by legislation or because customers want quiet machines and will choose a rival product for its lower noise level.

A machine buyer will not select a quiet machine without good reason. Those good reasons exist but they have got to be dragged out into the light of day. Even then legislation will be needed
15   before the majority of those responsible will do anything.

The real problem is basic: lack of knowledge. The effects of noise are not fully understood and some people refuse to believe it can have an adverse effect on hearing. Perhaps more important, though, is the fact that most design engineers forget
20   about it. There should be a poster displayed in every design office asking "What about noise?". It would cost a few pounds perhaps if an acoustician is summoned to look at the drawings but then the product will be quiet initially. It is cheaper to build in quietness than to take everything to bits later to try and rectify
25   matters.

Noise R Taylor

Questions

1   Here are some words and phrases from the passage. Give a word or phrase for each that could *replace* it in the passage:

techniques (line 2)
manufacturer (line 3)
strides (line 5)
benefit (line 6)
employ (line 7)
endeavour (line 9)

compelled (line 10)
legislation (line 10)
adverse (line 18)
summoned (line 22)
initially (line 23)
rectify matters (lines 24–5)

2   Put the following extracts from the passage into your own words:

is going to pursue quietness simply for philanthropic reasons (lines 3–4)
keep within the limits of airport noise regulations (lines 7–8)
choose a rival product (line 11)
they have got to be dragged out into the light of day (lines 13–15) before the majority of those responsible will do anything (line 15)
The real problem is basic: (line 16)
to build in quietness (lines 23–25)

■ *Exercise 3 Comprehension*

Read the following passage and answer the questions:

English has borrowed words from almost every language spoken. Anyone who doubts that claim should thumb through a dictionary which gives derivations, checking the origins of words like caravan, café, vodka and alligator. English speakers have travelled to all parts of the planet and found new objects and new ideas and, very sensibly, taken the native words to describe them.

Some of the borrowing has been more passive. The Viking raids of the tenth century and the Norman conquest led to great invasions of new words. The Vikings gave us such words as sky and skirt while the Normans transformed the language with hundreds of words showing their cultural variety. Recently the dominant influence on our language has been the United States. The main reason for this dominance is probably the sharing of a common tongue which makes communication easy and any new word or expression is quickly recognised and acquired. In addition, the United States is one of the major powers of the modern world which gives great status to its language. To use an American expression is to share in American prestige. Against this flow is set the force of reaction which denounces Americans as crude. The flow, however, has been going on for a long time and often purists will attack recent borrowings but use imports of the past. Many who complain that "teenager" is vulgar, will use "girlfriend" happily. Those who explode at the word "gimmick", will ask for a "battery" at the garage with no distaste.

It is generally safe to leave borrowing to the good sense of those who speak the language. If needed, words will be borrowed. If the need persists the words will stay and become familiar. If a borrowed word proves unpopular or unnecessary, it will be shed with no mourning. Usage is the judge. To challenge usage is rarely profitable and never sensible.

Questions

1 Make a list of words which English has borrowed.

2 Why has English borrowed words from other languages?

3 From which languages has English borrowed words?

4 Why does a borrowed word stay in the language?

5 How have words from other languages come into English?

■ *Exercise 4 Comprehension of a factual passage*

Read the following passage and answer the questions:

As the Second World War moved towards its grand finale, so the situation on mainland Europe grew ever more bloody. Mobile and efficient means of inflicting death were being used with greater accuracy and skill, and still more sophisticated
5 methods of destruction were being put into production. It was a time of horror, havoc and change.

The atmosphere in rural England, however, made a complete contrast, and apart from the blackouts and the patriotic duties of "Dad's Army", life went on untroubled and at the same pace
10 as it had for generations. In fact the only real difference between war and peace was that financially conditions were much better while hostilities lasted; for it was, and still is, a belief held by the farming community, both man and master, that "they" only care about farming during a war – a view that is not entirely
15 without foundation.

Farms were still a mixture of small fields and copses, or arable and pastoral, of horsepower and manual labour. The technical advances that had been made to mete out death had not yet been translated into new ways of relieving the burden of work and
20 combating the elements.

It was on a typical farm in south-west Cambridgeshire that I was born in 1943; the result of a union between a butcher turned farmer and a farmer's daughter turned teacher. I was delivered blue and crying, having tried to enter the world sideways; not
25 in a farmhouse but in a small semi-detached cottage, where I joined a brother and sister.

Our water was pumped by hand, outside the scullery window, and the bucket lavatory was across a small concrete path – a journey which to a small boy on a raw winter's night was both
30 frightening and cold. The garden was like most country gardens at that time, with daisies flowering in the lawn and a vegetable patch near the back door where marrows seemed to swell to gargantuan proportions. Silver birch, apple and plum trees grew in abundance, as well as a caterpillar tree that every summer
35 attracted hordes of black and red hairy caterpillars. Hens scraped busily at the bottom of the garden, where elms stood like guard-

ians of peace. The home was a happy place, the natural projection of a romance that had started when my mother was twelve and my father was thirteen. The exchange of love letters, sweets
40 and stolen kisses, had grown into the setting up of a home and the rearing of a family. Mother, at four feet eleven and three-quarter inches, had energy far in excess of her height and all day long she bustled here and there, cooking, sweeping, collecting eggs, singing hymns and humming. Fine old country smells
45 wafted through the house, chutney, jams, pies and sometimes home-made bread, and not a scrap of food was wasted. During her childhood mother had experienced hard times; fatherless at the age of ten, she had been brought up to count the pennies.

The Decline of an English village R. Page

Questions

1 What differences had the war made to farming?

2 What differences would the war make to farming in the future?

3 What were the occupations of the author's parents?

4 Give words or phrases to replace the following in the passage:
    sophisticated (line 4)   abundance (line 34)
    hostilities (line 12)   guardians (line 36)
    foundation (line 15)   wafted (line 45)

5 Explain the following extracts using your own words:
    seemed to swell to gargantuan proportions (lines 32–33)
    the natural projection of a romance (lines 37–38)
    had energy far in excess of her height (line 42)

6 Which of the author's parents was older, and by how much?

7 Give a brief description of the garden of the house where the author was born. Use your own words.

8 Why did the author's mother not waste food?

9 What was the author like at birth, and why?

10 On the evidence of this passage, do you think the author had a happy childhood?

2 Language: punctuation

Full stops

The most important punctuation in a sentence is the **full stop, question mark** or **exclamation mark** that ends it. You must show where one sentence ends and the next begins.

The full stop is the most common way to end a sentence. Here is a short paragraph of five sentences with the full stops left out:

> It was nearly time for the door of the huge store to open Mrs Jerome looked at her watch and tensed herself expectantly the queue behind her stretched over a hundred yards down the street in a few seconds, she would be exchanging the money clutched in her hand for the mink coat seductively displayed in the window her week of waiting would be made worthwhile

It is hard to read. You ask questions. Will the doors open Mrs Jerome? Does the queue stretch that far in a few seconds? Of course, you can work out the meaning but it is a puzzle, not a piece of writing.

A bad mistake is to use commas instead of full stops. Commas *cannot* do the work of full stops. A comma does not show that the sentence is over.

■ *Exercise 5 Using full stops*

The following passage needs *six* full stops. Put them in the right places.

> Mr Jerome had been given a power drill for Christmas it was easy to see that his present had not been left idle in one corner of the sitting room was a shelf he had fixed to the wall the shelf was shaky and inclined to the horizontal at a substantial angle but it was definitely attached around it were numerous holes of varying diameter these seemed to be Mr Jerome's early efforts to control his new weapon.

People do not usually have problems with full stops in speech. They pause naturally at the end of sentences. "Listen" when you are writing, so you "hear" where the full stops come. If it is possible, read aloud what you have written. That might help you to "spot" the full stops.

■ *Exercise 6 Commas or full stops?*

Some of the commas in the following passage are doing their job but others are at the ends of sentences. Replace the latter group with full stops:

> In the Town Square, under an affable sun, there was a smartly dressed lady testing consumer response to a new margarine, she would watch passers-by and, when she spotted an apparently willing soul, she would pounce, her selection, however, went sadly awry when she picked Una Carson, Una Carson was not a willing soul, despite the sweet calm of her face, Una was as stubbornly cantankerous as a donkey with earache, the market researcher, confident of an easy victim, smiled at Una, Una smiled back, it was a lovely smile but, to anybody who knew Una, it was a warning to leave town fast.

Punctuation, like any part of writing, can be improved by reading. When you read, check where the full stops come. As you become more aware of how writing is punctuated, you will have fewer difficulties yourself.

■ *Exercise 7 Using full stops*

Put full stops where they are needed in this passage:

> A local station was blaring out the charts in the kitchen mixed with the regular throb of the washing machine upstairs Julie's latest pop idol sang loudly while she accompanied him on her drum kit Dad was glued to the wrestling on TV with the volume full up and from the garden came sporadic explosions George was practising with his air rifle the various sounds merged into a hideous row the cat sat on a chair in the hall she was snoozing peacefully it was amazing that a creature could sleep in such a Bedlam.

Question marks

A question mark ends a sentence which asks a question. Like a full stop, it is followed by a capital letter. Here is a short paragraph where both full stops and question marks are used:

How can you justify this action? A by-pass where you suggest would mean demolishing many homes. Some people who live in that area, have been there since the war. They would have to be moved miles away. Established families would be split, decent folk cut off from their roots. Can that be right?

Question marks are used only at the end of direct questions, not those that are reported. A question mark is correct at the end of this sentence:

Why are you painting the cat red?

but would be *wrong* at the end of this sentence:

He asked me why I was painting the cat red.

In the first case, the question is being asked but in the second example someone is talking about a question asked previously.

■ *Exercise 8 Questions marks or full stops?*

Complete these sentences with either a question mark or a full stop.

a) He wanted to know where the camel had been
b) Why are we waiting
c) The constable wants to question you about your rear light
d) Joel must know why the fish pond has disappeared
e) Inspector Bloggs asked me how I had obtained the gold bar
f) How can you run a supermarket with no trolleys
g) Which is the knee that has been causing problems
h) Tell me why you do not like tapioca
i) Do you understand what I am saying
j) You have buried Uncle George, haven't you

■ *Exercise 9 Question marks and full stops*

Put full stops and question marks where needed in the following passage:

Have you seen the new woman at 26 she certainly thinks a lot of herself I saw her in a fur coat on Monday although it was sweltering hot do you know where she comes from somebody said she has been living abroad that could be true because she is very tanned have you heard her voice it is so upper-class she sounds as if she has the whole plum tree in her mouth I am not fooled though I can see straight through her she has something to hide do you get my meaning Lily reckons she is no better than she ought to be she may have been in prison she certainly goes red whenever a policemen passes what do you think

Exclamation marks

Another way to end a sentence is the exclamation mark. It is used after genuine exclamations like:

> Goodness gracious!
> What a pity!
> Shut up!

Exclamations are complete even if they do not have a verb. They are more common in speech so you will use the exclamation mark mostly in dialogue (or conversation).

Sometimes an ordinary sentence is surprising enough to have an exclamation mark. For example:

> He dived three hundred feet into a bucket of water!

Do **not** put exclamation marks at the end of unremarkable sentences like:

> We had a great deal of roast beef and carrots.

You need only *one* exclamation mark to emphasise a sentence. Exclamation marks lose their force if used frequently.

■ *Exercise 10 Exclamation marks*

Which five of the following ten sentences deserve exclamation marks?

a) The dog turned green and exploded!
b) Grandma was very unpleasant to me!
c) Arthur painted the room a beautiful shade of turquoise!

d) She picked up the Mini with one hand and tossed it over the wall!

e) What a mess!

f) He scored three goals in twenty-five minutes!

g) Rubbish!

h) She is determined to get to the very top!

i) The magician said he would saw a lady in half and he did!

j) Bonzo is the most adorable little puppy!

■ *Exercise 11 Full stops, question marks and exclamation marks*

Put full stops, question marks and exclamation marks where needed in this passage:

Have you bought a ticket for the circus it is truly amazing I have been to hundreds of circuses in my life but this is the best what a circus miracles take place in the big top I have been six times yet I am still lost in wonder at the spectacle the trapeze act leaves me gasping with fear one man hangs by his teeth a hundred feet above the ring and spins at an incredible speed there is no safety net and I can assure you that the whole audience sat spellbound what bravery think of the hours of rehearsal needed to get such mastery he has probably broken many bones in practice would you like to be a trapeze artist perhaps you would prefer lion taming that circus has a great woman lion tamer she is fearless there are lions, tigers and panthers in the cage with her but she is as relaxed as she might be at home what calm the climax of the act is breathtaking she lies on a bed of tigers, embracing a panther with her head in the mouth of a huge lion the other cats sit and watch they were as impressed as I was

3 Comprehension: imaginative passages

A comprehension exercise based on imaginative writing will be a
little different from one based on a factual passage. You may also be
tested on your interpretation of what you read. You might, for
example, be asked to guess what sort of work a character does and to
give reasons for your guess. There will probably be no clear
statement of what the job is so you will have to work like a detective
gathering clues. Your notes from the passage might be:

> He is described as muscular.
> He has hard calloused hands.
> His face is very tanned and he knows a lot about nature.
> He mentions a friend who is a shepherd.

and your answer might read like this:

> I think the man could be a farm worker. His physical description
> fits with an outdoor life and his knowledge of nature confirms
> that view. He mentions a friend who is a shepherd which makes
> my suggestions more likely.

Model comprehension exercise

Here is a comprehension exercise based on a passage from a novel.
Read the passage and the suggested answers to the questions with
the notes on how the answers were obtained:

> She knew by now her enemies in the class. The one she hated
> most was Williams. He was a sort of defective, not bad enough
> to be classed as such. He could read with fluency, and had plenty
> of cunning intelligence. But he could not keep still. And he had a
> 5 kind of sickness very repulsive to a sensitive girl, something cun-
> ning and etiolated and degenerate. Once he had thrown an inkwell
> at her, in one of his mad little rages. Twice he had run home out of
> class. He was a well-known character.
> And he grinned up his sleeve at this girl-teacher, sometimes
> 10 hanging around her to fawn on her. But this made her dislike
> him more. He had a kind of leech-like power.
> From one of the children she took a supple cane, and this she
> determined to use when real occasion came. One morning, at
> composition, she said to the boy Williams:
> 15 "Why have you made this blot?"

"Please miss, it fell off my pen," he whined out, in the mocking voice that he was so clever in using. The boys nearly snorted with laughter. For Williams was an actor, he could tickle the feelings of his hearers subtly. Particularly he could tickle the

20 children with him into ridiculing his teacher, or indeed, any authority of which he was not afraid. He had that peculiar gaol instinct.

"Then you must stay in and finish another page of composition," said the teacher.

25 This was against her usual sense of justice, and the boy resented it derisively. At twelve o'clock she caught him slinking out.

"Williams, sit down," she said.

And there she sat, and there he sat, alone, opposite to her, on

30 the back desk, looking at her with his furtive eyes every minute.

"Please, Miss, I've got to go on an errand," he called out insolently.

"Bring me your book," said Ursula.

The boy came out, flapping his book along the desk. He had

35 not written a line.

"Go back and do the writing you have to do," said Ursula. And she sat at her desk, trying to correct books. She was trembling and upset. And for an hour the miserable boy writhed and grinned in his seat. At the end of that time he had done five

40 lines.

"As it is so late now," said Ursula, "you will finish the rest this evening."

The boy kicked his way insolently down the passage.

The afternoon came again. Williams was there, glancing at

45 her, and her heart beat thick, for she knew it was a fight between them. She watched him. During the geography lesson, as she was pointing to the map with her cane, the boy continually ducked his whitish head under the desk, and attracted the attention of the other boys.

50 "Williams," she said, gathering her courage, for it was critical now to speak to him, "what are you doing?"

He lifted his face, the sore-rimmed eyes half-smiling. There was something intrinsically indecent about him. Ursula shrank away.

55 "Nothing," he replied, feeling triumph.

"What are you doing?" she repeated, her heartbeat suffocating her.

"Nothing," replied the boy, insolently aggrieved, comic.

"If I speak to you again, you must go down to Mr Harby,"
60 she said.

But this boy was a match even for Mr Harby. He was so persistent, so cringing, and flexible, he howled so when he was hurt, that the master hated the teacher who sent him more than he hated the boy himself. For of the boy, he was sick of the sight.
65 Which Williams knew. He grinned visibly. Ursula turned to the map again, to go on with the geography lesson. But there was a little ferment in the class. Williams's spirit infected them all.

The Rainbow D H Lawrence

Questions

1 *How do you know that Ursula expects trouble and is ready for it?*
The answer to this question is in the first few lines of the extract where you learn that Ursula has "enemies" in the class, particularly Williams. He has already "thrown an inkwell at her". Ursula hates him. She expects a confrontation so she gets the "supple cane" ready. The information suggests an answer like this:

> Ursula expects trouble because she has enemies in the class. Williams is a particular problem and she loathes this cunning, repulsive boy. A confrontation seems near but she is ready with a cane and the determination to use it if needed.

2 *How does Williams's behaviour rouse Ursula's anger against him?*
Ursula's anger builds up due to Williams's behaviour between line 15 and the end of the passage. The sequence of events is:

> He blots his book and is cheeky when questioned.
> He tries to slink out of his detention.
> He does very little work while he is kept in so she gives him another detention for the evening.
> In the afternoon he is insolent to Ursula.
> His influence unsettles the whole class.

Your answer might be:

> Ursula gives Williams a detention. He tries to slink out but
> she catches him and sets him to work. He does so little that
> she orders him to stay in after school. In the afternoon, he
> is insolent to her and his influence unsettles the class. Ursula
> was angered by his cheek and fearful that he might turn the
> whole class against her.

3 *Why was there little point in Ursula sending the boy to Mr Harby,
the headmaster?*
Lines 61–64 provide the answer. Williams is a "match" for Mr
Harby because the boy screams so much when hurt. Any teacher
who sends Williams to the head will be "hated" for doing that.
The suggested answer is:

> There is little point because Mr Harby disliked dealing with
> the boy who made a huge fuss when punished. The head-
> master hated any teacher who sent Williams to him.

4 *In what ways does the author try to make us dislike Williams? Refer
in your answer to both his appearance and his personality.*
Williams's cunning and temper are mentioned at the very beginning. His appearance is described at "etiolated" which means
"unhealthily pale". The boy "whines", "slinks" and "is mocking".
His insolence is stressed regularly. His eyes are "sore-rimmed".
There is something "indecent" about him. He is "cringing and
flexible". The picture is of a cunning, animal-like boy. A possible
answer is:

> Williams is presented as a pallid, fish-like creature, almost
> unnatural in appearance. The boy is called a "beast" and has
> no good qualities. He can be violent but mostly his manner
> is furtive and cunning. He is insolent because he thinks that
> Ursula is too scared to act against him. The whole picture of
> Williams makes a reader feel disgust and revulsion.

5 *What do you learn of Ursula's personality from the passage?*
On line 5, Ursula is described as "sensitive". She is "determined"
in line 13 and line 25 shows her acting against "her usual sense of
justice". The rest of the extract deals with the conflict between her
determination and her sensitivity. The suggested answer is:

Ursula is a sensitive person very upset by Williams's behaviour which makes her forget her normal sense of justice. She shows determination to face the problem presented by Williams but her will is undermined by the powerful effect the boy has upon her.

6 *Do you think Ursula would make a good teacher eventually? Use evidence from the passage to justify your answer.*
Whether you answer "yes" or "no" is unimportant as long as you back up your opinion. If you answer "no", your evidence from the passage could be:

Teachers should not hate pupils. (line 1)
She is too sensitive. (line 5)
Corporal punishment is wrong. (line 12)
Ursula is unjust because of her hatred of Williams. (line 25)
Teachers should deal with their own pupils not send them to the head. (line 59)

This evidence could produce this final answer:

Ursula will not make a good teacher because she is too sensitive. Teachers should not hate pupils but Ursula hates Williams and her hatred makes her treat him unjustly. She clearly intends to use the cane which a good teacher would not need to do and she threatens to send Williams to Mr Harby. Successful teachers can deal with their own pupils.

■ *Exercise 12 Comprehension of an imaginative passage*

Read the following passage and answer the questions:

Piff was a small, or supposedly small, invisible friend that Polly had acquired when she was about five. And while she lasted she was a great nuisance.

One would start to sit down upon a conveniently empty chair
5   only to be arrested in an unstable and inelegant pose by a cry of anguish from Polly, one had, it seemed, been about to sit on Piff. Any unexpected movement, too, was liable to bowl over the intangible Piff who would then be embraced and comforted by

a lot of sympathetic muttering about careless and brutal daddies.
10 Frequently, and more likely than not when a knockout seemed
imminent, or the television play had reached the brink of its
dénouement, there would come an urgent call from Polly's
bedroom above; the cause had to be investigated although the
odds were about four to one that it would concern Piff's dire
15 need for a drink of water. We would sit down at a table for four
in a café, and there would be agonised appeals to a mystified
waitress for an extra chair for Piff. I would be in the act of
releasing my clutch when a startling yell would inform me that
Piff was not yet with us, and the car door had to be opened to
20 let her aboard. Once I testily refused to wait for her. It was not
worth it; my heartlessness had clouded our whole day.

Piff, for one of her kind, had been remarkably diuturnal. She
must have been with us for the best part of a year – and it
seemed a great deal longer – but in the end she somehow got
25 mislaid during our summer holiday. Polly, much taken up with
several more substantial, and much more audible, new friends,
dropped Piff with great callousness, and she was still missing on
our return journey.

Once I was satisfied that she was not going to follow and take
30 up residence with us again I was able to feel quite sorry for the
deserted Piff, apparently doomed to wander for ever in summer's
traces upon the forlorn beaches of Sussex; nevertheless, her
absence came as a great relief – even, one suspected, to Polly.

Chocky John Wyndham

Questions

1 Who was Piff?

2 In what ways was Piff a nuisance to the writer?

3 When and where did Piff finally disappear?

4 What reasons does the writer give for Piff's disappearance?

5 Why does the writer feel sorry for Piff in the end?

6 Without using figures of speech, re-state *in your own words* the
  following extracts from the passage:
  arrested in an unstable and inelegant pose (line 5)
  the television play had reached the brink of its dénouement
  (line 11)
  my heartlessness had clouded our whole day (line 21)

7 For each of the following words give a word or phrase that could
  be used to replace it in the passage without changing the
  meaning:
  imminent (line 11)
  investigated (line 13)
  mislaid (line 25)
  callousness (line 27)
  residence (line 30)
  forlorn (line 32)

4 Words: learning new words

The best way to learn new words is by reading. As you read, you meet new words. Look up any unfamiliar word in a dictionary and write it with its meaning in a special notebook. Use the word fairly soon in speech or writing. Then use it again so it becomes one of *your* words. The best way to learn new words is:

1 Read the word
2 Look up the word
3 Note the word
4 Use the word

Using a dictionary

You should have a good-sized dictionary published recently. Pocket versions do not always give enough details. Dictionaries go out of date as new words arrive, old words depart and some words change meaning. A dictionary published before 1950 will not contain "astronaut" or "beef burger"!

A good dictionary gives a lot of interesting information:

The meaning of a word – many English words have several meanings and you may have to search to find the meaning that fits.

The spelling of a word – you can usually track a word down if you know the first three letters.

The pronunciation of a word – some words sound very different from the way they look. Dictionaries show you how to say a word.

Where a word comes from – English words often come from other languages.

■ Exercise 13 Using a dictionary

Look up the following words in a good dictionary. Find their meanings, pronunciations and from which languages they come.

masquerade, maverick, clairvoyance, zest, panorama, anonymous, rogue, phenomenon, lank, arc.

Word groups

A way to learn new words is in groups which might have some **connection**. The link helps your memory. Here is a list of words which could describe a person's face, features or complexion:

sallow	wan	rubicund	mottled	ravaged
alabaster	hirsute	reptilian	cavernous	desiccated

These are useful words for describing a character's appearance. Check all meanings and note the words in your book, if necessary.

■ Exercise 14 Colour words

Everybody knows the common colour words – red, yellow etc. – but here are some less common ones. Try to use them in speech and writing.

scarlet	vermilion	aquamarine	indigo
maroon	saffron	azure	emerald
crimson	russet	magenta	sepia

A good way of describing colours is to put two words together with a hyphen between – dove-grey, brick-red. The first word tells you the exact shade of the colour. You can make up your own examples: beer-brown, custard-yellow.

■ Exercise 15 Hyphen colours

Here is a list of everyday colours. Put a word in front of each to describe a particular shade of colour. For example: ladybird-red

red	white	yellow	grey	black
pink	orange	blue	brown	green

■ Exercise 16 Meeting new words

Pick out all the words in the following passage that are new to you. Look them up in a dictionary and put them in your notebook. Try to use them soon.

> The old man was ecstatically agitated. Despite his manifest age, he advanced with ostentatious vigour. His emaciated hands waved extravagantly and the quavering voice was exultant. He was too articulate. The words had no individual identity. They were a mere confusion of sound. It was impossible to guess what had caused this effervescence. Perhaps he had discovered an elixir of life or unearthed a treasure of inestimable worth. The incoherent gabble emanating from his desiccated lips gave no clue to the cause of his immoderate excitement.

5 Spelling: double letters

There are five letters in the alphabet which are called *vowels* – a, e, i, o, u. All the rest are known as *consonants*. Vowels can have a *short* sound or a *long* sound. In certain words the sound of the vowel gives a guide for spelling. Look at this list of words:

winner   chatter   cutting   trotted   wettest

In each word the vowel in **bold** type has a *short* sound and is followed by a *double* consonant. Now look at a second list:

lining   later   meter   duty   motor

In these words the vowel has a *long* sound and is followed by a *single* consonant. So the guide is:

After a short vowel sound, double the consonant.

■ *Exercise 17 Single or double consonants?*

Choose the correct spelling in the following sentences:

a) A roten/rotten decision by the umpire stoped/stopped us winning/wining.
b) He was siting/sitting on the beach writing/writting a leter/letter.
c) The liner/linner steamed out into the Chanel/Channel.
d) He droped/dropped the papers/pappers into a mudy/muddy puddle/pudle.
e) I was hoping/hopping that you would stop biting/bitting your nails.

This spelling guide is a useful reminder but there are words which do not follow the guide.
Some consonants need to be looked at specially.
x is *never* doubled.
v is *very rarely* doubled e.g. navvy.
c is *rarely* doubled e.g. soccer, tobacco.
k is *very rarely* doubled e.g. chukkah, trekking. You usually write **ck** instead.

Compare these two lists:

wicket	hiking
bucket	fluky
locker	choker
backward	baker

The vowels in **bold** type in the first list have *short* sounds and are followed by **ck**.

The vowels in **bold** type in the second list have *long* sounds are followed by **k**.

■ Exercise 18 ck, k or cc?

Fill the gaps in the following passage with -ck-, -k-, or -cc-:

Mr Jones stopped work at the ba___ery and washed because he was sti___y. He left, lo___ing the door behind him. He bi___ed home to a meal of roast chi___en. After eating, he filled his pipe with toba___o and lit it. He enjoyed smo___ing after a meal. In the afternoon, he went to a so___er match. He had bought the ti___et from a friend who preferred cri___et.

6 Exercises for revision

■ Exercise 19 Comprehension: a factual passage

Read the following passage and then answer the questions, *using your own words* as far as possible.

Do better locks really stop burglars?

Have you taken to heart all those warnings to "Lock It"? Have you put strong locks and bolts on your doors and windows and do you make sure they are all secure whenever you go out? Well the Home Office, the government department in charge of these
5 crime prevention campaigns, has got news for you. It has decided that it is not going to make much difference to your chances of being burgled. The revelation comes in a new study from the department's research and planning unit: *Residential Burglary* by Stuart Winchester and Hilary Jackson. Its principal conclusion,
10 which will embarrass the Home Office officials responsible for crime prevention policy, is that good security is a poor deterrent to burglars.

The report says that the most important influence on a burglar's choice of target is the ease with which the house can
15 be approached unobserved. The most vulnerable houses are set well back from the road; those hedges, shrubs and fences that people put up to give themselves privacy also assist burglars.

The other key factor is whether the house is occupied. Four out of five daytime burglaries and 19 out of 20 evening break-
20 ins take place when there is nobody in. Only at night is the burglar likely to call when you are at home, but night-time burglaries account for only fifteen per cent of break-ins.

When the burglar has got both time and privacy in which to work, only the toughest security measures will be effective. Most
25 burglars are willing to force a door or window and to break glass to get inside. Only iron bars or steel doors seem to be able to withstand a determined burglar. This means, say the Home Office researchers, that to concentrate crime prevention resources in the present way, on what is called "target hard-
30 ening" can make only a small impact.

Burglary is one of Britain's commonest crimes – the average household now has a one in 35 chance of being burgled in any one year. About half a million homes suffer every year and though the cash value of what is stolen is frequently small the
35 psychological impact of the crime is often severe.

It is difficult to catch burglars because they rarely leave fingerprints and are almost never seen by their victims. Official figures claim that just under a third of burglaries are eventually cleared up, but when unreported burglaries are included, the
40 true figure is probably nearer to a sixth. As a result, the police and Home Office concentrate on preventive measures. The Home Office runs national crime prevention publicity campaigns, while at local level there are some 500 full-time police crime prevention officers. The new study – in a thriving
45 tradition of Home Office research that pours cold water on official policy – challenges the underlying rationale of this work.

One useful innovation might be burglary squads – either of police or local residents – on patrol. This method has produced good results in Seattle, USA, but a disadvantage is that people
50 tend to lose interest, especially when the rate of burglary is as low as it still is in most parts of Britain.

Sunday Times

Questions

1 Give words or phrases which could replace the following words in the passage.
   principal (line 9)
   unobserved (line 15)
   withstand (line 27)
   severe (line 35)
   eventually (line 38)
   innovation (line 47)

2 What are the main reasons for a burglar choosing a particular house to break into?

3 Explain the following extracts from the passage using your own words:
   good security is a poor deterrent to burglars (lines 11–12)
   to concentrate crime prevention resources in the present way (lines 28–29)

the psychological impact of the crime (lines 34–35)
challenges the underlying rationale of this work (line 46)

4 What is meant by the phrase, "target hardening", used in the passage?

5 Why is it hard for the police to catch burglars?

6 Summarise, in a short paragraph, all the statistics about burglary given in the passage.

■ Exercise 20 Putting in full stops

Put full stops where they are needed in the following passage:

It had been a very windy night overturned cars were everywhere several trees had been blown down one gigantic oak had demolished the statue of Boadicea the roof of the Corn Exchange lay in pieces on the road a lamp-post, previously upright, was now bent double and a bus stop, once outside the Corn Exchange, was a hundred yards up the road the traffic-lights had disappeared broken glass covered the pavements it was a scene of chaos

■ Exercise 21 Full stop or question mark?

Complete these sentences with either a full stop or a question mark:

a) Where has the new chef put the stuffed owl
b) I want to know what you are doing with that camel
c) Has the caretaker cleaned the floor with shoe polish again
d) Which is the twin with gout
e) Has Great Grandma said why she wants a rowing machine for Christmas
f) He asked me if I had heard the latest single by The Clan
g) Where has George hidden my wooden leg
h) Can you tell me why the landlord has stopped serving gorillas
i) Does the inspector care what has happened to my valuables
j) The hairdresser inquired why Joan did not want her hair tinted pink

■ *Exercise 22 Question marks, exclamation marks and full stops*

Put question marks, exclamation marks or full stops where needed in this passage:

> It has been a very strange week for Aunt Ada on Monday, she turned green do you know Aunt Ada she works at the chemical factory the doctor told her that the chemicals caused it he gave her some tablets they were green as well the doctor said they would work at once he's always optimistic, isn't he nothing happened for a couple of days though and she was getting very depressed then what do you think on Wednesday she turned blue of course she went straight back to the doctor he told her to keep taking the tablets they worked eventually by Friday, she was back to normal she didn't go to work all week I don't blame her, do you know she said she felt really off-colour.

■ *Exercise 23 Correcting punctuation*

The following passage has a number of full stops, question marks and exclamation marks in the wrong places. Correct the punctuation of the passage.

> You're a disgrace. You walk round the streets, looking like a scarecrow! Do you care. Six months ago, you were a man with some pride? Look at yourself now! Your hair is dirty and matted? That coat you're wearing should be in the dustbin! Why don't you answer. Has the cat got your tongue! I will never understand how your mind works? There's no reason for you to act like this! Norah's a good wife, isn't she. The children lovely! What a mess. What a rotten mess? I hope you feel ashamed! Can you feel any more. I doubt it! Get out of my sight? Do you hear. Get out.

■ *Exercise 24 Comprehension of imaginative passage*

Read the following passage and answer the questions:

> It had seemed quite easy to Hale to be lost in Brighton. Fifty thousand people beside himself were down for the day, and for quite a while he gave himself up to the good day, drinking gins

and tonics wherever his programme allowed. For he had to stick
5 closely to a programme: from ten till eleven Queen's Road and
Castle Square, from eleven till twelve the Aquarium and Palace
Pier, twelve till one the front between the Old Ship and West
Pier, back for lunch between one and two in any restaurant he
chose round the Castle Square, and after that he had to make
10 his way all down the parade to West Pier and then to the station
by the Hove streets. These were the limits of his absurd and
widely advertised sentry go. Advertised on every Messenger
poster: "Kolley Kibber in Brighton today". In his pocket he had
a packet of cards to distribute in hidden places along his route:
15 those who found them would receive ten shillings from the
Messenger, but the big prize was reserved for whoever chal-
lenged Hale in the proper form of words and with a copy of the
Messenger in his hand: "You are Kolley Kibber. I claim the
Daily Messenger prize."
20   This was Hale's job, to do sentry go, until a challenger
released him, in every seaside town in turn: yesterday Southend,
today Brighton, tomorrow _____.
   He drank his gin and tonic hastily as a clock struck eleven,
and moved out of Castle Square. Kolley Kibber always played
25 fair, always wore the same kind of hat as in the photograph the
Messenger printed, was always on time. Yesterday in Southend
he had been unchallenged: the paper liked to save its guineas
occasionally but not too often. It was his duty to be spotted –
and it was his inclination too. There were reasons why he didn't
30 feel too safe in Brighton, even in a Whitsun crowd.
   He leant against the rail near the Palace Pier and showed his
face to the crowd as it uncoiled endlessly past him, like a twisted
piece of wire, two by two, each with an air of sober and determined gaiety. They had stood all the way from Victoria in
35 crowded carriages, they would have to wait in queues for lunch,
at midnight half asleep they would rock back in trains an hour
late to the cramped streets and the closed pubs and the weary
walk home. With immense labour and immense patience they
extricated from the long day the grain of pleasure: this sun, this
40 music, the rattle of the miniature cars, the ghost train driving
between the grinning skeletons under the Aquarium promenade,
the sticks of Brighton rock, the paper sailor's caps.

Brighton Rock Graham Greene

Questions

1 For each of the following words give a word or phrase that could replace it in the passage without changing the meaning:

absurd (line 11)   inclination (line 29)
distribute (line 14)   immense (line 38)
hastily (line 23)
occasionally (line 28)

2 Explain, in your own words, the following extracts from the passage:
showed his face to the crowd as it uncoiled endlessly past him (lines 31–32)
each with an air of sober and determined gaiety (line 33–34)
they extricated from the long day the grain of pleasure (lines 38–39)

3 Why is Hale in Brighton?

4 Hale expects to be murdered while he is in Brighton. What clues are there in the passage to suggest he is in danger?

5 How did Kolley Kibber "play fair"?

6 Why did the Messenger not like to save its guineas "too often"?

7 Describe in your own words the day out in Brighton for one of the crowd on that Whitsun holiday.

■ Exercise 25 Using a dictionary

Find the meanings, pronunciations and origins of the following: words:

acumen, cove, cataract, etiquette, fjord, gratuitous, homonym, insinuate, jocular, kinetic, logic, misogynist, nostalgia, obsolete, pemmican, puttee, swarf, tumbril, voluble, zephyr.

■ Exercise 26 Using a dictionary

Find the following in your dictionary:

a) A word meaning "a wild Norse warrior", beginning ber-;
b) A word meaning "fortress", beginning cit-;
c) A word meaning "to reach highest point", beginning cul-;
d) A word meaning "the mouth of the river", beginning est-;

e) A word meaning "a picturesque cave", beginning gro-;

f) A word meaning "wise", beginning pru-.

■ Exercise 27 Using a thesaurus

Use a thesaurus to find twenty words to describe the weather.

■ Exercise 28 Learning new words

Look up any unfamiliar words in the following passage. Put the words and meanings into your notebook:

> The atmosphere was invigorating. Mrs Montgomery inhaled with obvious gratification. A vacation at this spectacular resort had been a real inspiration. A state of extravagant euphoria overwhelmed her so different from the customary depression. The breathtaking panorama which spread before her enraptured eyes almost mesmerised the senses. Mrs Montgomery ambled ecstatically along the promenade drinking in her novel environment. The azure sea undulated somnolently, merging with the tranquil blue of the sky. Birds, effortless aviators, hovered arrogantly on thermal currents. Mrs Montgomery ensconced herself on a strategically placed bench and gazed at a view of unblemished magnificence. She wondered what act of virtue had made her deserve such exorbitant pleasure.

■ Exercise 29 Single or double consonants

Choose the correct spelling in the following sentences:

a) She choped/chopped down the roten/rotten elm in a biting/bitting wind.

b) The new man in the team bated/batted well with a broken/brocken arm.

c) The draughtsman needed a finer/finner nib in his maping/mapping pen.

d) Mr Jones was reclining/reclinning on the filing/filling cabinet, siping/sipping his shery/sherry.

e) We were discusing/discussing important maters/matters but not deciding/decidding anything.

1 Summary: making notes

A summary question asks you to re-write a passage in fewer words, usually around a third of the original number, keeping the main ideas.

Qualities of a good summary

In your summary, the examiner is looking for:

1 fluent, direct writing
2 correct use of language
3 the essential points and arguments from the original passage
4 different vocabulary from the original
5 the exact number of words asked for (or very close to that).

Stages in writing a summary

A good summary is generally the result of careful preparation in which you:
1 read the passage thoroughly;
2 read it again, making notes in your own words;
3 write a rough draft of your version from the notes;
4 revise the draft to get the right length, using the original if needed;
5 write out the final version.
With experience, you may be able to leave out one of the stages but it will *always* be vital to read the passage thoroughly.

■ *Exercise 1 A spoken summary*

Read an extract about 400 words long from a newspaper or a book. Tell someone *briefly* what it was about, *using your own words*.

How to make notes

Making notes is important in summary work. You decide what is essential from the passage and put those ideas in your words. There are two points to make:

1 Your notes must *not* add new ideas to those given in the passage.
2 The main ideas of the passage may not be spread evenly. Some parts may be left out while other parts will be hard to reduce at all.

When you are making notes, there are two major ways of cutting down material:
1 leaving out examples;
2 putting a number of points under one heading. Look at this sentence:

> The Eskimoes have many ways of resisting the Arctic winter like rubbing blubber on their faces, wearing many layers of caribou skin, building up body fat and ensuring that their igloos are well-heated and insulated.

The writer gives four examples of the basic point. Your notes would omit the examples:

> Eskimos have various methods of keeping out the cold.

Here is another sentence:

> Gower late cut delicately, drove thunderously, hooked powerfully and pulled as though threatening to put the ball into orbit.

Gower's strokes are described in different ways but one note will cover everything:

> Gower batted well.

■ Exercise 2 Making notes from sentences

Put the following sentences into notes as suggested above:

a) In the Vatican library are ancient manuscripts describing the life of Christ, gospels beautifully illustrated by mediaeval monks and solid leather-bound examples of the first printed Bibles.

b) She poisoned thirteen elderly members of the Elvis Presley fan club, electrocuted a series of insurance salesmen, mowed down a whole football team with a shotgun and beheaded a maiden aunt.

It is useful to tackle the passage a paragraph at a time. Often your summary will have the same number of paragraphs as the original.

The polar bear is the most powerful bear. He can run faster than any human and regularly bounds over ice-hummocks higher than a man. He can climb the vertical sides of icebergs and leaps out of the water like a porpoise. An average adult weighs around half a ton with paws the size of dinner plates. Hunters claim that the polar bear always uses the left paw for any activity needing strength like killing a seal.   (77 words)

The paragraph could be reduced to the following notes:

Polar bear strongest of bears. (*repeats idea of first sentence*)
Good at running and jumping. (*ignores comparison and example*)
And climbing. (*leaves out leaping – included in "jumping"*)
Weighs about half a ton. (*copies passage*)
Huge paws. (*ignores comparison.*)
Left paw said to be stronger. (*leaves out who made "claim" and example*)

■ Exercise 3 Bad notes – good notes

Read the following paragraph and the two sets of notes. Say what is wrong with each set and then make your own notes.

In the past, women often took a job to earn a little extra for the family budget and to escape the home and meet new people. For the men, though, work was a major way to get enough money, status and relationships to justify life itself. When the older children left home, the woman got a job to replace the lost income. Her wages often proved a godsend if her husband retired or lost his job or was forced to take lower-paid work. Generally the work she did was well within her capacity and much like what she was used to at home. In the big cities the demand for cleaners, canteen assistants and dressmakers made it easy for her to find work.   (123 words)

a) Women wanted to get out of the house. Men wanted to even more. Wives' money helped with the housekeeping. Their work was easy. There was a lot of work available in the big cities.

b) In former days, females frequently sought employment for extra money to supplement the housekeeping. They also enjoyed the social contacts involved in work. Men, on the other hand, needed their work to give them financial and social confidence. As the family broke up, the woman's work helped to stabilise the family income. Her money was also useful if her husband's wages disappeared or were reduced. Normally her work was similar to that done at home and not over-demanding. There were plenty of openings for women in the big cities.

Model notes

Here is a complete passage for summary. Read it through and the notes and explanation given after it. The passage divides neatly into three paragraphs.

When children play in the street, they not only avail themselves of one of the oldest play-places in the world; they engage in some of the oldest and most interesting of games, for they are games tested and confirmed by centuries of children, who have played them and passed them on, as children continue to do, without reference to print, parliament, or adult propriety. Indeed these street games are probably the most played, least recorded, most natural games that there are. Certainly they are the most spontaneous, for the little group of boys under the lamp-post may not know until a minute before, whether they are going to play "Bish Bash" or "Cockarusha", or even know that they are going to play.

A true game is one that frees the spirit. It allows for no cares but those fictitious ones engendered by the game itself. When the players commit themselves to the rhythm of incident of "Underground Tig" or "Witches in the Gluepots", they opt out of the ordinary world; the boundary of their existence becomes the two pavements this side of a pillar box, their only reality the excitement of avoiding the chaser's touch. Yet it is not only the nature of the game that frees the spirit; it is the circumstances in which it is played. The true game is one that arises from the players themselves.

It may be argued that the value of a game as recreation depends on its inconsequence to daily life. In the game that adults organise for children, the outside world is ever-present. Individual performances tend to become a matter of congratulation or shame; and in a team game, paradoxically, responsibility presses hardest. The player who "lets down his side" can cheer himself only with the sad reflection that those who speak loudest about the virtues of organised sport are the people who excel in it, never the duffers. He is not likely to have been told that such a man as Robert Louis Stevenson felt that cricket and football were colourless pastimes compared with the romance of "Hide and Seek".   (349 words)

Children's Games in Street and Playground   Iona and Peter Opie

Notes (these are numbered for easy reference)
1 The street is one of the oldest play-grounds.
2 Children's street-games have been passed down for generations.
3 Those games are lively, spontaneous pastimes.
4 A good game lets loose a child's imagination.
5 Children become so involved that all else is forgotten.
6 The best games derive from the players themselves.
7 Children enjoy games which have no link with real life.
8 Games organised by adults often put pressure on children.
9 Organised games are most popular with those who succeed at them.

Notes 1–3 cover the main points of the first paragraph. Unimportant detail and specific examples are left out. Again in the second paragraph, three main points emerge. The first and last sentences get a note each but everything between is reduced to note 5. The third paragraph produces three notes too. Once more a first sentence merits a note on its own. This is not unusual. *First and last sentences of paragraphs are often important because they summarise the meaning of the paragraph.*

■ *Exercise 4 Changing a passage into notes*

Read through the following passage and change it into notes:

The lawn mower offers an excellent illustration of the strategy of upgrading the nation's concept of what is appropriate. A simple-minded, intensely rational person might assume that hand mowers would be increasingly popular today and that power mowers would be almost impossible to sell. After all, lawns are getting smaller all the time. And adult males are feeling more and more the need for physical exercise as they spend more time in sedentary, short-week jobs. They come home from the office beating their chests and growling for exercise. The situation that has developed, however, shows how dangerous it has become to try to anticipate consumer behaviour by the application of humourless logic, and ignoring the role marketing strategies may play.

The lawn-mower industry was able to convince American males that it was somehow shameful to be seen pushing a hand mower. And power mowers were promoted as a wonderful new gadget. Power mower sales rose seventeenfold in fifteen years! By 1960 more than nine out of every ten lawn mowers sold were powered. Such powered mowers cost from three to five times as much as hand mowers. Furthermore, having a mere motor on your mower was not enough in some neighbourhoods. You also needed a seat on it. Hundreds of thousands of American males began buying power mowers with seats. These, of course, cost ten times as much as a hand mower. A Midwestern auto-accessory chain began using a "save your heart" theme to promote sales of self-propelled power mowers. One trade journal reported that this merchandiser "makes it a practice to trade customers up into higher-priced units". And so the mower industry was able to keep its dollar volume rising in a most satisfying manner. Apparently more advances were still to come. *Newsweek* carried a prediction that in the future electronic lawn mowers would be sweeping over lawns on pre-programmed patterns without human attendants.   (312 words)

The Waste Makers Vance Packard

2 Language: making words agree

Subject and verb

In Unit one you met subjects and verbs. To remind you, here is a sentence with the subject and verb in **bold type**.

We (subject) **were eating** (verb) the beans in silence.

In this sentence the verb *agrees* with the subject, that is, the right part of the verb has been chosen for the subject. If the writer had written:

We was eating the beans in silence.

the subject and verb would *not agree*. This is a common error with verbs like: to be   to have   to do

◼ *Exercise 5 Subject – verb agreement*

Choose the right form of the verb in these sentences to agree with the subject:

a) It weren't/wasn't my fault.
b) He do/does argue a lot.
c) They is/are having a party.
d) I has/have finished my rice pudding.
e) If you is/are available, we have/has a chance.
f) I am/are convinced that you is/are a Martian.
g) They don't/doesn't seem like elephants.
h) They was/were quickly surrounded by gnomes.
i) It is/am a piece of prehistoric rhubarb.
j) Have/Has she drunk her carrot-juice today?

Agreement between subject and verb sometimes goes wrong because they are separated by many words. Look at this sentence:

Daisy, a delightful dancer and the darling of the discos, **do** a paper round to make ends meet.

The verb in **bold** type does not agree with its subject. The writer has made the verb agree with "discos", not "Daisy". The sentence should read:

Daisy, a delightful dancer and the darling of the discos, **does** a paper round to make ends meet.

■ *Exercise 6 Subject – verb agreement*

Make the verb in brackets agree with its subject in the following passage:

> It is nine o'clock. The most abject of the newcomers (cry) and the last of the parents (shuffle) out of the class. Some older children in the corner (play) happily. The teacher, wearing her first-day smile, (move) towards the little band. The bravest among them (smile) back, three of their number (stare) blankly at the green walls but the little girl, already in tears, (tremble) at the approach of this ominous lady and (howl). The teacher, conscious of her misgivings, (draw) back but to no avail. The reluctant pupil, yearning for familiar places, (race) from the room.

Either ... or, neither ... nor, whether ... or

Sentences which include the words – "either ... or", "neither ... nor", "whether ... or" – can cause problems of agreement. There are three simple rules to remember:

1 *If all the subjects are singular, then the verb is singular.*
2 *If one of the subjects is plural, then the verb is plural.*
3 *If pronouns are used, then the verb agrees with the nearest one.*

The following three sentences illustrate these rules:

> Either the warthog or the stick-insect *has* to go.
> Whether John or the twins *do* it is unimportant.
> Neither he nor I *am* guilty.

In the first sentence "either" could be left out. The rule would not change. The third sentence, although correct, is awkward. It would be better to write:

> Neither of us is guilty.

■ *Exercise 7 Subject – verb agreement*

Make the verb in brackets agree with its subject in these sentences:

a) I don't care whether you or he (go) to the cinema.
b) Neither the generals nor the Prime Minister (know) the answer.
c) A rose bush or a rhododendron (make) an attractive display.

d) (Have) either the baker or the milkman called recently?
e) Either the beefburgers or the egg (smell) awful.
f) Neither the purple dress nor the yellow dungarees really (suit) me.
g) Either *the Mail* or *the Mirror* (be) acceptable.
h) Neither you nor he (understand) my problems.
i) Radiators or a gas fire (heat) the room equally well.
j) Whether she or he (win) does not matter.

Singular *not* plural

Here is a list of words which are singular but are sometimes treated as plural:

anyone anybody   everyone everybody   no one nobody
someone somebody   either neither

Here is a sentence with two mistakes caused by treating "everybody" as plural:

> Everybody in the town **have** worked out **their** own views on the matter.

The words in **bold** type are wrong. The sentence should read:

> Everybody in the town **has** worked out **his** own views on the matter.

The word "his" covers both male and female in this case.

Exercise 8 *Singular or plural?*

Choose the correct word in these sentences:
a) Neither is/are capable of making up their/his mind/minds.
b) Anybody know/knows how to lace his/their shoes.
c) Everybody do/does their/his own washing-up.
d) I don't think anyone care/cares about my bunions.
e) We will give everyone the right to own their/his house.

Collective nouns

Collective nouns cover a number of people or things. Examples are:

choir (of singers)   fleet (of ships)   flock (of sheep)

Usually such words are singular but if you want to talk about the differences in a group, you can treat a collective noun as plural. You could write:

> The flock of sheep made **its** way across the field.

with "flock" seen as singular but, on a different occasion, you could write:

> The flock **were** scattered and some of **them** bleated piteously.

The plural forms – **were** and **them** – show that the "flock" is not seen as a single unit.

■ *Exercise 9 Singular or plural?*

Choose the correct words in the following sentences:

a) The committee were/was unanimous in its/their decision.
b) The pack of cards was/were scattered and we never found them/it all.
c) The crowd started fighting among itself/themselves.
d) The team do/does not combine well because it/they trains/train apart.
e) The government have/has completed its/their programme.
f) The gang have/has split up and it/they has/have gone to various countries to live on the profits of their/its crimes.

"have" *not* "of"

Two more common mistakes are dealt with in this section. The first is the confusion of "of" with "have".

This happens because the two words can sound alike. Say "should have" and "some of" aloud. Both words become "erv". This leads to sentences like this being written:

> I should **of** done it if I had known.

This is wrong. It should read:

> I should **have** done it if I had known.

Which part of the verb?

Another confusion produces incorrect sentences like this:

He **done** it all for money.

The writer has mixed up two parts of the verb "do". This is what should have been written:

He **did** it all for money.

Well-behaved verbs like "lift" do not give this problem. While "do" can change to "done" or "did", "lift" changes only to "lifted".

Some people write as though all verbs behave as "lift":

We **singed** the song and now we have **singed** every song in the book.

This should be:

We **sang** the song and now we have **sung** every song in the book.

Here are some other verbs that do not behave like "lift":

I see	I saw	I have seen
I grow	I grew	I have grown
I eat	I ate	I have eaten
I tear	I tore	I have torn

▋ Exercise 10 The right part of the verb

Choose the correct words in the following sentences:

a) We done/did a terrible deed.
b) I comed/came, I saw/seed, I conquered.
c) Have you buyed/bought my tin of chocolate grasshoppers?
d) I digged/dug the whole field before I went/goed to the club.
e) The dog has eaten/ate the gorilla's sandwich.
f) Mildred ringed/rang/rung the bells yesterday.
g) She has ringed/rang/rung those deafening bells for years.
h) The Borgias' guest drunk/drinked/drank his wine suspiciously.
i) They have not sended/sent my pension even though I wrote/writ.
j) I took/taked a photo of her when she had growed/grew/grown an extra foot.

3 Summary: the final version

Writing up

The last job in summary is to write up your notes in fluent English using the number of words specified.

Here is a paragraph to be summarised in 44 words. Read it and the notes following.

> Modern Japan is a very specialised society. From the moment he leaves school, a man will be steeped in the activities and ideas of his chosen profession. Communication between people in different professional groups tends to be at the purely social level because it is very hard to find a common language to discuss an unfamiliar area of specialism. A man finds it hard and probably does not wish to move freely from occupation to occupation because the effort is so great and the attachment to the first choice so strong. So professors do not become politicians, engineers stay engineers and accountants rarely venture out of accountancy. Some commentators insist that this pattern produces stability but others claim such a stability prevents the flow of ideas and could ultimately be bad. (131 words)

Notes

> Japanese society encourages specialisation. Man immersed in job from moment leaves school. Hard for people in different jobs to talk about work. Rarely change jobs – set in ways – retraining huge task. Stability or constraint of ideas? (36 words)

The notes can be expanded by only *eight* words in the write-up. Here is the suggested final version:

> Japanese society encourages specialisation. A man is immersed in a career from leaving school and thus finds it hard to talk with people in other occupations about work. Changing jobs is rare. Some see this as stability while others view it as social stagnation. (44 words)

■ *Exercise 11 Summarising a paragraph*

Summarise the following paragraph in 42 words:

Once a purely academic activity, archaeology is now big news. Even in the 1930s, a major newspaper bought the rights to reveal the contents of an Egyptian tomb while another funded a dig on a Roman site in North Wales. The advent of television, however, has brought the thrill of archaeology into the homes of millions and archaeologists are now media people, displaying their finds and explaining their craft to a huge and clearly fascinated audience. Some of their colleagues have seemed sceptical even critical of such exposure but this view is hard to defend. The evidence of history is surely the heritage of all not a chosen few. Archaeologists have a social duty to inform as well as a scientific duty to preserve.   (124 words)

Model summary exercise

Below is an example of a full-length passage for summary in 120 words:

We are supposed to be living in an epoch in which television has supplanted radio. Yet as long as radio exists at all, the take-over can never be quite complete. It is impossible to feel the same respect for the younger medium. Radio, after all, has glorious things in its history. Not only has it pioneered many important developments in education but it has an heroic dimension. Brave men, hiding in barns and attics, have defied tyranny by means of radio. Its equipment is cheap, portable and easy to hide; that of television is complex, heavy and costly. The Gestapo in occupied Europe were effectively hindered and baited by means of radio, and if the miniature transistor set had been invented in those days, the resistance might have been even more formidable. Television will never come to the aid of freedom in this way. A pirate television set is an impossibility; its whereabouts would be spotted before the equipment was half set up. Again, radio can work *for* the law as well as against it. As an infant medium it showed that it meant business by securing the arrest of the murderer Crippen aboard an Atlantic liner.

By comparison, television has nothing to show except the

closed-circuit scanning of department stores. It belongs, irredeemably, to the world of merchandise. That is why commercial television seemed a natural, if depressing development; whereas a commercial radio network seems the debasement of something noble, like those circus acts where lions jump through hoops of paper.

If radio is murdered, it will be an inside job. The medium will be overshadowed by television, but never eclipsed altogether, so long as radio "to itself do rest but true". What this boils down to is that the sound-broadcasting side of the BBC must be no further humiliated and pestered by the forces of commercialisation. For as long as we can remember, the BBC has given us the best sound-radio services in the world, and although the dismantling has already gone very far, we must, as a nation, firmly insist that it shall go no further.   (347 words)

John Wain

Here are notes on the passage (numbered for reference):

1 TV supposedly taken over but radio still commands respect.
2 Radio's great past – educational innovation and support for freedom.
3 Helped brave men resist dictators.
4 TV could not do this – too bulky and expensive.
5 Radio also helped law when a new invention.
6 TV naturally commercial medium – radio not.
7 Radio will survive if it maintains quality BBC famous for.
8 Radio must be preserved and protected from commercial pressure.

There are 65 words in these notes. This leaves plenty of words to spare. If your notes are too brief, it might mean that you have cut too much and you will need to refer to the original before writing up. Here is the suggested final version:

Today television is supposed to have taken over from radio but radio still commands more respect.

Radio, in its great past, has contributed to educational innovation and also given support to freedom. It has helped men resist dictators. Television could never do this because its equipment is too costly and bulky. In its infancy, too, radio showed its potential to help the law when Crippen was apprehended.

Television, of course, provides security systems in big shops. It is a naturally commercial medium, ideally suited to advertising, whereas radio seems debased by such intrusion.

Radio will survive if it stays true to itself and maintains that quality that has been the BBC's hallmark. It must be protected from commercial pressure. (120 words)

The vocabulary is sufficiently different from the original. Some words like "radio" and "television" cannot be changed. In all, the summary shows that the writer:

* understands the original
* can pick out the essential points
* can write up those points in good English, using a set number of words.

■ Exercise 12 Summarising a passage

Summarise the following passage in 120 words:

In the first half of the Victorian age, poor people in the great cities were less cut off from the country than the already endless miles of bricks and mortar might suggest. The contacts were (and remained) closer in the industrial north and midlands than within the vast metropolitan complex; yet, in the sixties, East End slum dwellers north and south of the river went out to work as field labourers in the market gardens, and what would in time be considered quaintly rustic crafts – basket weaving and the like – were carried out in the slum courts of Bethnal Green with materials gathered on Essex marshes and farmland.

Animal husbandry was a common urban pursuit: besides innumerable draught animals, dairy cattle were kept in the biggest cities, and at the mid-century one could find grimy pigs rooting about alleys in the City of London as well as among the middens of inner Manchester. Until the livestock market was moved in 1855, a considerable area in the heart of the capital had, with its leather-gaitered, felt-hatted dealers and drovers, much of the air of a busy – but exceptionally unpleasant – country town. A variety of poor people were constantly shifting in and out of the main centres of population, some leaving the towns to make long, slow foot-journeys through the countryside.

Paradoxically, as the century went on the improvement in communication, especially in rail transport, tended to promote the estrangement of town from countryside by reducing the number of people – waggoners, drovers, wandering traders, showmen, craftsmen and labourers – who lived more or less amphibiously between the two.

Much of the mobile population was thoroughly disreputable, and its shuttlings had a significant bearing on the economy of the underworld. Altogether, any attempt to survey the seamy underside of mid-nineteenth-century life would be futile without some look at the various migrants dotting the white metalled highroads – now almost deserted by the stage coaches, post chaises and great ship-like long distance carriers' waggons that recently had passed along them.   (333 words)

The Victorian Underworld Kellow Chesney

4 Words: saying it briefly

Brief messages

Writing summaries is not the only time you need to be brief. In a tele-message words cost you money. A tele-message like the following could make you bankrupt.

> Dear Mum,
>   I am coming home this weekend after all. It was quite a hard decision to make because there are one or two things I need to do here but I have decided that they can be left to next week. I shall catch the nine o'clock train from here on Friday night and get in at ten o'clock sharp. I look forward to seeing you then.
>   All my love, Jill

All Jill needed to say was:

> Mum, coming home 10 pm train this Friday, Jill.

The essential facts are given, as in the notes for a summary.

■ *Exercise 13 Same meaning in fewer words*

Re-write the following tele-message in only 10 words:

> Dear Mum,
>   You will be glad to hear that Jill had twin girls this morning. It was quite a shock as you can imagine because the hospital had never mentioned the possibility of twins. The doctors and nurses looked a bit surprised too. Anyway, we are both very thrilled. Jill and the babies are doing well. She sends all her love and wants to know if you can think of another name!
>   Love, Bill

One word for many

Almost any piece of writing can be reduced. That does not mean it is bad writing but sometimes using too many words makes writing awkward and hard to follow. Look at this sentence:

> I stopped work due to the fact that I was tired.

The phrase "due to the fact that" is clumsy. It is better to write:

> I stopped work because I was tired.

■ *Exercise 14 One word for many*

Replace the words in **bold** type in these sentences with *one* word, keeping the meaning.

a) I am going to talk **on the subject of** left-hand screwdrivers.
b) The cost should be **in the region of** £5,000,000.
c) My parsnips will be ready **in the near future**.
d) I hope he **answers in the affirmative**.
e) **In the event that** you are on Mars, come and see us.
f) Colmswater is a little village **in the neighbourhood of** Kendal.
g) We should be able to fix your brakes for **a figure less than** £50,000.
h) **At the present time**, lemmings are in short supply.
i) I am not **in favour of** topless Members of Parliament.
j) The chimpanzee was destined to become the next **occupant of the White House**.

Sentences can often be made more concise without loss of meaning. This is helpful especially when you are doing a summary.

■ *Exercise 15 Reducing sentences*

Cut the following sentences as much as possible without loss of meaning:

a) I paid out a great deal of money while I was buying things in town.
b) The water level got higher and higher until the river flowed over its banks and covered the neighbouring fields.
c) I had a talk with the man who lives in the house next to ours.
d) The sweet old lady punched the man who had broken into her house to steal her valuables and he dropped unconscious.
e) The craft which had been designed to travel in space rose from the ground and climbed upwards.
f) The new tenant of No 10 Downing Street left the door open a little.

Brief descriptions

Writing succinctly is a useful skill. Here is the description of a short-lived job:

Hired. Tired. Fired.

That says a lot in three words. Here is a selfportrait in under 30 words:

Tall and skinny, that's me. The hair and eyes are brown, mouth and ears are big. Somebody said I've got my Mum's nose. She can have it back.

■ *Exercise 16 Brief descriptions*

Describe one of the following in less than 30 words:

a) a particular animal or species
b) a shop where you go regularly
c) a picture or a photograph

5 Spelling: making words plural

General rule and exceptions

The *general rule* to make nouns plural is to add an -s.
dog dogs   ceiling ceilings   joke jokes
There are *exceptions:*

1 *nouns ending in -s, -ch, -sh, -x, and -z and -o* add -es in the plural:

boss bosses witch witches   sash sashes
box boxes   topaz topazes   potato potatoes

Some nouns ending in -o follow the general rule:

cello cellos   solo solos   disco discos

2 *nouns ending in -f or -fe* change the -f or -fe to -ves in the plural:

wife wives   half halves

some nouns in this group follow the *general rule*:

chief chiefs   roof roofs   dwarf dwarfs

3 *nouns ending in -y* change the -y to -ies in the plural:

country countries   fairy fairies   fly flies

But those ending in -oy, -ay, -ey just add -s:

boy boys   day days   monkey monkeys

4 *some nouns form unusual plurals.* They have to be remembered:

child children   goose geese   mouse mice
man   men/woman women

5 *some nouns stay the same* in the plural:

sheep sheep   salmon salmon   deer deer

6 *some nouns are always used in the plural:*

scissors   trousers   measles

■ *Exercise 17 Plurals*

Give the plurals of the following words:

ash, window, turkey, louse, mackerel, billiards, diary, ditch, proof, tooth, knife, tomato, class, commentator, cuckoo.

Combination nouns

The plurals of "combination" nouns – nouns made up of words joined together – can cause problems. There is no rule but here are some examples:

girl-friend girl-friends   hanger-on hangers-on
brother-in-law brothers-in-law   woman-doctor women-doctors

Foreign nouns

Some of the "foreign" words in English keep their "foreign" plurals, while others obey English rules. A few have a "foreign" and an English plural. Here are some examples:

appendix   appendices, appendixes
axis   axes
criterion   criteria
formula   formulae, formulas
fungus   fungi, funguses
genius   geniuses
index   indices, indexes
octopus   octopuses
stimulus   stimuli

The plural of the French word Monsieur is Messieurs. This word is rarely used in English but it is found in an abbreviated form in business addresses:

Messrs T and L Brotherton, Ltd

6 Exercises for revision

▪ *Exercise 18 Summarising sentences*

Summarise these sentences in less than one-third the number of words:

a) Collecting stamps from different countries of the world is a most enjoyable hobby which can lead to a greater knowledge of those countries, a great awareness of colour and design and sometimes to the thrilling discovery of a rare and wonderful stamp worth a great deal of money.   (48 words)

b) It is very hard for you to know if you are buying a bargain at your local supermarket because the wide range of package size on offer makes it almost impossible to work out the best buy unless you have a higher degree in mathematics or a portable personal computer.   (50 words)

c) The British weather is an eternal topic because it is one of the most important elements in the life of this society, a variable which adds the flavour of unpredictability to every occasion, turning the summer picnic to Noah's flood or transforming grey February streets with the glorious gold of sunshine.

(51 words)

▪ *Exercise 19 Improving a bad summary*

Read the following paragraph. The summary below has a number of faults. What are they? Produce your own version avoiding these faults.

Our Sun is not unique. It is just one of a huge number of similar stars spread through the vastness of the universe. Something like 200 billion stars can be seen with the most powerful telescope on Earth and there are certainly many more beyond our sight. Each of these stars, like the Sun, is a mass of energy radiating heat and light, and they range in size from bodies smaller than our Earth to those bigger than the whole solar system. Nobody can tell if these other suns have planetary systems. Our telescopes are not strong enough to show this detail but it is likely that systems like our own are scattered widely across space. It is also likely that some of those planets circling remote stars have the conditions to sustain life. We may not be alone in the universe.

(142 words)

Summary (Number of words allowed – 50)

Our Sun is not unique. It is just one of a lot of similar stars in the big universe. 200 billion stars are visible through powerful telescopes from earth and there could be a lot more than that. Each of these radiates heat and light like the Sun. Some of them have planets with life. (56 words)

■ *Exercise 20 Summarising a passage*

Make a summary of the following passage in 120 words:

There is no doubt that shopping as it is today will be revolutionised in the near future. The change will be caused by that maker of modern miracles – the computer. A shopper will sit in a comfortable chair and push some buttons on his or her personal computer. Perhaps he or she will work systematically, checking the different brands of a particular item, or possibly the shopper will window-shop, picking things at random until one takes his or her fancy. Whatever the approach, the goods that interest you, the shopper, will be displayed on a monitor screen with details of specification and price. You will be able to get more information by typing in questions. Finally, after full consideration, you will make your choice through the same computer keyboard. No money will change hands; the computer will debit your account. The whole process will be swift and painless.

The benefits of this system are great. There will be no need to travel miles by car or venture out in rain or snow. All the trials of parking will be avoided and the tiring walk loaded with heavy parcels. There will be no battling through crowds to the counter and if one shop is out of stock, then a quick tap on the keyboard will show where the required item *is* available.

Admittedly the goods could cost a little more because they will have to be delivered. The added expense, however, could well be covered by savings on travel and it is likely that prices generally will be lower because shops will economise on premises and staff. The number of consumers could well increase because shoppers will not be confined to stores in their neighbourhood. Identical choice will be offered to the consumers of Perth and Penzance.

People who enjoy shopping in its present form might see disadvantages in the computerised approach. Perhaps a few old-fashioned centres will be kept for such eccentrics but for the great majority who find present-day shopping stressful and frustrating, the future offers the chance to enjoy shopping in a new form. The time saved can be filled with genuine recreation.

(354 words)

■ Exercise 21 Verb agreement

Fill in the gaps in this passage with any verb that agrees with the subject:

Her face ...... incredibly wrinkled. Lines ...... everywhere across the dried skin so it ...... like earth cracked by drought. She ...... not crying but her eyes ...... watering and little drops ...... down her face along paths which the wrinkles ...... Despite her age, her gaze still ...... purpose. It ...... steady almost piercing as though experience ...... her to see into people's hearts. The veins on her hands ...... out blue and hard. She ...... her coat around her as she ...... along. Some young lads ...... sight of her and ...... her shambling walk. They ...... no harm but she ...... them and ...... out a single word of abuse. The rebuke ...... the boys and they ...... still looking ashamed and perhaps a little fearful too. Stories of spells and witches ...... still fresh in their young memories.

■ Exercise 22 Verb agreement

Choose the right form of the verb in these sentences:

a) The panda or the polar bear is/are on the poster.
b) George does not care whether Villa or City are/is winning.
c) Either the elves or the goblin with the limp is/are to blame.
d) Neither he nor I have/has seen the gasworks by moonlight.
e) Tell me whether the awful twins or their vile uncle want/wants to come.
f) The black beans or the blue cheese gives/give the best flavour.

■ *Exercise 23 Brief descriptions*

Describe one of the following in about 40 words. Write in sentences.
a) your favourite television programme
b) a book you have enjoyed
c) a room in the house where you live
When you have finished, see if you could reduce the number of words without loss of meaning.

■ *Exercise 24 One word for many*

Cut down the following passage by replacing groups of words with a single word where possible. The target is 57 words (perhaps you can do better).

Mrs Dupont's sons and daughters got together in the hall. There was a considerable number of them, in the region of four score, or so it seemed to the man who had dealt with the family's legal affairs. This gentleman, who had lived a long time, placed himself upon a chair and let his eyes travel round the room. On the face of everybody was the desire for money. Mrs Dupont's statement of how her estate should be divided lay in front of the venerable figure. He took the document in his hand, coughed a single time, then communicated the contents of the document to his audience.

■ *Exercise 25 Plurals*

Change the words in **bold** type into the plural:

The **man-at-arms was** standing by the **dairy**. **He was** looking at **his wife** who **was** digging up **a potato**. **A sheep** stood in the **field** waiting for the **dwarf** and the **fairy** to come and look at **her foot**. **A witch** flew by on **her broomstick**. **She was** having **octopus** and **fungus** to eat that night. **Her child** had cut the **fungus** with **scissors**.

UNIT FOUR

1 Letters: to friends and relations

Personal letters should communicate in a lively, interesting way. To succeed, you should ask yourself two questions:

1 Why am I writing?
2 Who is going to read what I have written?

What you write to ask a favour of your uncle will be very different from a description of a party to your best friend.

Postcards

A familiar example of the personal letter is the holiday postcard. Here are two cards from Joe who is on holiday in Italy.

Venice, 8.8.84

Dear Harry,

Here is the view of the Grand Canal I promised you. You're lucky it can't convey the smell. I am enjoying the holiday after the traditional day locked in an Italian loo (graffiti by Leonardo da Vinci). The weather is fantastic and so are the local girls, especially Giovanna – but I won't make you jealous. Eating carefully after the tummy trouble. I never want to see another plate of spaghetti again.   Joe

---

Venice, 8.8.84

Dear Grandma,

I hope your weather at home is as good as we're having here. It's really hot and I'm soaking up the sun. Do you like the view of the Bay of Naples at sunset? The colours are superb. Italy is a beautiful country. Coming to Venice is like going back in time. I took a trip in a gondola. It was expensive but the best way to see the sights. The gondolier didn't sing. Singers cost double. Look after yourself.

Love, Joseph.

Each card refers to the same holiday but what is included depends on who will be reading the card. Harry will be amused by the tummy upset and curious about "Giovanna". The second card, however, avoids Joe's gastric problems and his amorous escapades. They might worry Grandma. Joe keeps to safe ground and even signs himself "Joseph".

■ Exercise 1 Holiday postcards

Write a holiday postcard to each of the following people:

a) a friendly teacher who used to take you for history at school;
b) a married elder sister who lives away from home;
c) Dad.

What to write about in a letter

Some people find ordinary letters difficult to write because they think everyday life is dull. They are wrong. Each day is different. Here is a list of "ordinary" events which could be put into a letter.

Meeting an old friend
Buying some clothes
Being late for work
Visiting someone or somewhere
Hearing a record for the first time

These are general headings. For your letter you would add some details like this:

Met George Turner – first time in three years – borrowed a pound!
Bought shirt in sale – Mum said the colour makes her feel sick.
Saw Liverpool for the first time – they lost.
Enrolled in Car Maintenance evening class – fed up with garage bills.
Decided to paint picture – inspired by Italian holiday.

■ Exercise 2 What to write about in a letter

Write a list of things that have happened to you in the last fortnight.

Dear Harry,

Thanks for the last letter – longer than usual, wasn't it? That's why I'm late answering. I've just finished reading it.

Your news about the engagement was a shock. Your letter sounded cheerful though so I'll believe you when you said it was the right thing to do. You can buy me two pints now you're not saving.

Who do you think I saw last week? George Turner. He's the same as ever – all old jokes and oily smiles. He says he's making a bomb selling "high-class goods" to the "upper set". Mind you, he still borrowed a pound from me. I never learn.

Last weekend I saw Liverpool play for the first time. A chap from work gave me a lift up there. I felt like a kid with my scarf and rosette. You know what happened? They lost at home for the first time this season. Still, it was great on the Kop, swaying and singing. Did you see me on TV?

I've made two resolutions for autumn. First, I'm going to paint a big picture on my bedroom wall. My Italian holiday inspired me. I got CSE1 in Art and I'm sure Mum will love the idea! I'm not sure what to paint yet. Any serious suggestions?

I've also signed on for an evening class in Car Maintenance. Dad takes the car to Logie's Garage and old Logie fleeces him. After the course, I'll do the servicing and repairs. It'll be handy when I get my own motor too.

I bought a smart shirt in the sales. It cost a mere £2. Mum's a bit rude about it. It is rather a vivid green but it grows on you. Mum says it gives her heartburn. The little brother likes it though. His taste must be improving.

Talking of bargains reminds me. You wanted to know where I got my hi-fi. I looked around but, in the end, I bought the equipment from Sadlers in Cheam. They were the cheapest place by pounds.

That will do. I'm keeping you from drink and football.

All the best,

Joe

When you write a letter to a friend, you not only give your news, you also respond to the last letter from that friend. You might:

1 answer a question
2 react to a special piece of news
3 provide particular information

Joe is writing to his friend Harry using the details given before Exercise 2. He is responding to Harry's last letter by:
 i) reacting to Harry's news that his engagement has broken up;
ii) telling him of a cheap place to buy hi-fi equipment.

Joe's letter is opposite.

■ *Exercise 3 Letter to a friend*

Write a letter to a friend. Include five things that have happened to you recently and respond to two points in your friend's last letter to you.

Asking a favour

Sometimes a personal letter can be quite formal. If you are asking a favour, you may have to make your case clearly. Here is a plan for a letter to an aunt asking her to guarantee a Hire Purchase agreement:
 i) a general introduction
 ii) a statement of the request
iii) an idea of what is involved
iv) a promise to behave responsibly
 v) a final paragraph
From those notes the final version on page 102 was produced.

96 Laurel Terrace,
Manchester
MA9 8QP
13th September 1984

Dear Aunt May,

Thanks for the card from Greece. It must be sweltering in August. Did you manage to see the sights?

As you probably know, I'm buying a motorbike. Since the buses were cut, it's impossible to get into town after 6.30. I'm doing two evening classes next year so I'll need transport.

I'm getting the bike on Hire Purchase which means having a Guarantor to sign the agreement. It has to be somebody who knows me well. Mum and Dad are too closely related to me but the salesman said an aunt would be acceptable so would you act as my Guarantor?

As you work in a bank, you'll know what being a Guarantor involves. If I don't keep up the payments, then, in theory, they could come to you for the money. The man in the garage says that rarely happens. Usually, the bike is taken back and sold to cover the outstanding debt.

I hope you know me well enough to know that I wouldn't get in arrears. I promise to be very responsible about this debt and pay each monthly instalment directly I get my wages.

I hope you'll agree but if you feel you can't, I'll try and find someone else. Give my best wishes to Uncle Jack. Mum says she hopes you'll visit us when you're down here in November.

All the best,
Harry

Exercise 4 Letter to a friend or relative

Write one of the following letters to a friend or relative.

a) Asking somebody to be your referee for a job
b) Apologising for forgetting an important appointment
c) Agreeing that a *clumsy* friend can borrow a precious possession

2 Language: punctuation

The comma

The punctuation mark that causes most bother is the comma. The comma divides sentences to make them easier to understand. You do the same thing in speech when you pause. In fact, if you read aloud a piece of writing, that will often show you where commas are needed. A common use of the comma is to bracket off a part of the sentence. Here is an example:

The lumberjack, who was struck by a giant redwood, fell silent.

The words between the commas add to the main sense. The sentence would be complete as:

The lumberjack fell silent.

but the writer wants to make it clear *which* lumberjack "fell silent" so the extra information is given.

Usually these added words need two commas in the same way that brackets have to be opened and closed. If, however, the addition comes at the beginning or end of a sentence, one comma is enough. You would write:

Far from being cold, Tuesday was the hottest February day since 1863.

with one comma because the added words come at the beginning of the sentence.

◼ *Exercise 5 Commas*

Add one or two commas where needed to each of these sentences:
a) We saw Aldershot my favourite team lose in the final.
b) The bishop in the opinion of PC Johnson had murdered the maid.
c) Although nobody else could hear them the guns kept her awake.
d) The postman despite his wooden leg fathered twenty-three children.
e) Aunt Mabel who loves crab paste has a habit of walking sideways.
f) The giraffe was left here so Mother tells me by a passing circus.

Commas are used when someone is spoken to. Here are two examples:

> I wonder, Mr Tudball, if you would mind knocking before you enter?
> Mr Tudball, never do that in this office again.

Lists need commas as well. Leaving them out can alter the meaning. The following two sentences are the same except for a comma but they have different meanings.

> Fred bought milk chocolate and eggs.
> Fred bought milk, chocolate and eggs.

Even when the sense is clear without commas, it is easier to follow a list if the commas are included.
When you write a sentence like:

> In his pocket the boy had a piece of string, a broken penknife, two lumps of sugar and some chewed gum.

which contains a list, it is up to you whether you put a comma after "sugar". The other commas are compulsory but that one is optional.

■ *Exercise 6 Commas*

Add commas where they are needed in these sentences:

a) I am not going to tell you again Henry.
b) She grows red roses white roses yellow roses and sprouts.
c) You can have egg and chips fish and chips steak and chips or just chips.
d) Look here Alice what are you playing at?
e) During the evening she drank a bottle of wine three tots of rum a glass of port ten cans of beer and the water in the goldfish bowl.
f) Well Mr Wotherspoon why did you paint the budgie pink?

Sometimes you use a number of sentences in a list. Look at this sequence:

> The dog barked. He snarled. He barked again. Finally he lay down by the door.

This is really a list of the dog's actions. You could leave the sentences as they are or combine them with words like "and". The best way is probably to use commas and make one "listing sentence":

The dog barked, snarled, barked again and finally lay down by the door.

■ *Exercise 7 Commas*

Add commas where needed in these sentences:

a) Paint the garage feed the hamster mend the cleaner and cut the grass.
b) Mum brought a pipe-rack Dad a tea cosy Aunt Maud a stale cake and George donated a litre of onion wine.
c) I was punched trampled on kneed in the ribs and left in the gutter.
d) She got up early left her corn flakes ran all the way to the station and still missed the train.
e) Ian can't do it David can't do it Leroy can't do it but *I* can do it.

■ *Exercise 8 Commas*

Add commas where needed in the following passage:

Although it was December the weather was hot and Miss Allenby the postmistress wore a summer dress bought in 1956 to the party. Miss Allenby an ample lady of sixty was rarely so rash. Her motto derived from experience was "never trust the weather" but despite this cautious philosophy she donned a flimsy creation which would normally have appeared during the occasional heatwave of July or August. Mind you Miss Allenby was not alone in this reckless gesture. Mrs Timms from the Laurels Miss Mack old Elsie Jones and even tiny Miss Pecksniff the doctor's great-aunt turned out their lightest clothing seduced by the unseasonable temperature.

The semi-colon

The semi-colon indicates a longer pause than the comma. It is used to link sentences which are strongly related. For example:

> He had a mean streak; he would never give to charity.

A full stop could replace the semi-colon. The writer chooses the semi-colon because it keeps both statements in *one* sentence to emphasise the link.

The following show the two common errors made with semi-colons:

i) She will come in Spring; when the weather improves.
ii) She is very capable; and she deserves her promotion.

In (i) the semi-colon should be replaced by a comma. The words after the semi-colon are not a complete statement and the semi-colon can be used to link complete statements only.

In (ii) the two statements are linked in two ways – by the semi-colon and by "and". One of the two should be left out.

It is also possible to link a number of statements using semi-colons if they are strongly related and you do not want to use full stops. It is correct to write:

> My husband is very ill; he eats nothing; his face is haggard; he lies on his bed as though awaiting an inevitable death.

Semi-colons cannot link statements which are not strongly related. Full stops are needed then.

■ Exercise 9 Semi-colons

Which of these sequences of sentences could be linked by using semi-colons?

a) The trainer was disgusted with her swimmers' times. She had an idea. She put a shark in the pool. That speeded them up.
b) She looked at him. He was wearing tartan trousers. They revealed about ten centimetres of puce sock and even pucer leg.
c) They must be looked after. They deserve our help. They cannot be left homeless.
d) I had just arrived when the phone rang. It was my brother. He lives in Australia. I did think of joining him but I hate kangaroos.
e) He was worried. The problem grew. It monopolised his thoughts. He was obsessed.

The colon

The colon can do three jobs in a sentence.

1 *It can introduce a list*:

For Lent I gave up: washing up, tapioca and ice-cold baths.

2 *It can show that what follows in some way explains what has gone before*:

The scene was total confusion: duchesses floundered in custard, generals paddled in gravy and smart young chaps sat bewildered in mashed potato.

3 *It can divide a sentence into two balancing parts*:

The vegetables were slightly burnt: the meat was incinerated.

■ *Exercise 10 Colons*

Put colons where they are needed in this passage:

Life is hard my wife has left me, the dog has distemper and I have lost my watch. Yesterday was bad today is worse. There are basic problems shortage of money, lack of influence, deathwatch beetle and dandruff. I might sign on for an evening class. Three possibilities suggest themselves Bulgarian poetry, yoghourt-making and bowls. Knowledge makes the full man ignorance leaves him empty.

■ *Exercise 11 Commas, semi-colons and colons*

Put commas, semi-colons and colons where needed in this passage:

The marrow Mr Smith's pride lay great green and gleaming in the hothouse. He put his success down to three things cold tea soot and rabbit droppings. Although he hated getting up early he would rise at five to feed the vegetable. According to Mr Smith dawn feeding was essential. The marrow was drenched with tea it was powdered with soot its roots were nestled in rabbit manure. Some thought Mr Smith had divine powers others believed he was in league with Satan. Now like an anchored airship it reclined under Mr Smith's fatherly gaze proof of his loving care. He would win the cup at the show his marrow would gain the red rosette success would be his. Certain of victory Mr Smith who rarely showed emotion gave a slight smug smile.

3 Letters: writing formally

Formal letters are very different from the letters you send to friends or relatives but the principle is the same. You write to interest and inform your reader. You do not write in a pompous, complicated way. Precise, simple language is needed with careful planning beforehand.

Address and date

All formal letters have an address for answers which is set out in the top right-hand corner of the first page with the date of writing below. There will also be, on the left-hand side, an "inside address" – a copy of the address on the envelope. Here is a normal layout:

144 Acacia Avenue,
Brickhill,
BEESTON,
Dorset WY21 8NB
14th September 1985

Mac-Fi Ltd,
Thistle Trading Estate,
GLASGOW
GL3 4BZ

Starting the letter

How to start the letter depends on whom you are writing to. There are three possibilities:

1 *If you are writing to a particular person – like the editor of the local paper – but you do not know that person, start*:
   Dear Sir,   *or*   Dear Madam,

2 *If you are writing to a firm with no idea who will read the letter, start*:
   Dear Sirs,

3 *If you are writing to a person you have met a few times, start*:
   Dear Mr Brown   *or*   Dear Mrs Smith

The beginning of the letter is a greeting and stands on a line of its own. The letter proper starts on the next line.

Ending the letter

When the letter is finished, there are special ways of signing off which must match that first greeting.

Yours faithfully If you started Dear Sir, Dear Madam or Dear Sirs, you end Yours faithfully and put your signature underneath.
Yours sincerely If you started Dear Mr Brown, or Dear Mrs Smith, you end Yours sincerely, and put your signature underneath.

Always print or type your name and title under your signature.

■ *Exercise 12 Beginning and ending a letter*

You are writing to your dentist, Mr Stewart. You see him regularly for check-ups. Write your address for the letter and how you start and finish.

Complaint letters

One type of formal letter is the complaint. Imagine you have bought a collapsible bicycle by mail order. It arrives with one pedal bent. Here is a possible plan for your complaint letter:

Date of order – accompanied by cheque
Date of receipt of bicycle
Pedal bent – everything else fine
Send replacement pedal quickly – going on holiday
Will return damaged pedal if wanted – refund of postage?

which could be written like the letter on page 110.

Your ref: A3Z/89

The Old Mill,
Fetters Lane,
WINGATE,
Hants PO16 7MD

14th August 1986

Nu-Bike Ltd,
20–24 Kettering Road,
NORTHAMPTON,
Northants NO3 8LL

Dear Sirs,
   On June 24th I ordered a collapsible bicycle from you.
With the order I sent a cheque for £99.95
   The bicycle arrived by carrier yesterday and today I
unpacked and assembled it according to the instructions.
Unfortunately, one of the pedals is badly bent. Everything
else is in good order.
   Please send a replacement pedal quickly. I go on holiday
soon and I want to take the bicycle with me.
   I will return the damaged pedal if you want it, and if you
agree to refund the cost of postage.

Yours faithfully,
Bernard Unwin

This letter is brief and to the point. It would be easy to make it
longer and more complicated but that would waste time and could
cause confusion.

■ *Exercise 13 Complaint letter*

Write a complaint letter based on one of the following situations. Make a brief plan first and check that your letter is clear and direct.

a) You have reserved a seat for a rail journey. On the train you find all the seats taken and that no reservation has been made for you.
b) You buy a tin of meat on holiday. You do not open it until you get home when you find that the contents are mouldy.
c) After one week in a new house, the paint starts peeling.
d) There is a council waste-bin outside your home which has not been emptied for weeks. It is smelling and attracting flies.

■ *Exercise 14 Complaint letter*

Write a complaint letter based on one of the following topics. Make a plan first.

a) You buy goods from a mail order firm. You have had problems – wrong items sent, money lost, abusive letters etc.
b) You regularly support a football club but in the last year the ground facilities have got very bad despite a doubling of the entrance fee.
c) Your postal service has become very inefficient – late delivery, letters put in wrong house, letters apparently opened etc.

Letters to a newspaper

Another type of formal letter is written to a newspaper for publication. The letter is addressed to the editor but the writer hopes to inform or persuade the readers. The following is a typical example:

53 Dunster Gardens,
MURCHESTER MU3 7NK

24th March 1987

The Editor,
Murchester Guardian,
MURCHESTER

Dear Sir,
I have recently started a Murchester branch of the Society for Widows. Our first meeting is at the Guildhall on Sunday April 10th at 2.30 pm.

The Mayor and our local MP, Jane Jones, have kindly agreed to come. We hope also to have with us the founder of the Society, Mary Dempster.

The branch has no money as yet. We hope to raise the twenty pounds booking fee for the Guildhall by a collection at the meeting.

Murchester is a large town and there must be many widows living locally. Some will have lost husbands recently while others will have been alone for years. Do come to the meeting if you need help or feel you could give support to others.

Yours faithfully,
Lorna Dean (Secretary)

The plan for this letter would have looked like this:

First meeting – where and when
Important people coming
Getting money to pay bill
Encourage attendance

The letter on page 113 is proving a point. The writer supports his argument with evidence.

25, Cotham Park Road,
COGBOURNE CO4 7QW

3rd November 1986

The Editor,
Cogbourne Advertiser,
COGBOURNE

Dear Sir,

The street-lighting in the Cotham area is appalling. At night, any pedestrian is at risk and especially the old, the young and the disabled.

The pavements in Cotham are narrow and uneven. Walking was hazardous even when the council allowed us lighting but, in our present darkness, it is impossible to see the holes and bumps. I am an active man but last week, walking home late, I tripped on an uneven paving slab and broke an ankle.

My experience is not unique. I took a survey of my neighbours. Three described similar incidents. One lady collided with a lamp-post while taking her dog out at night.

Darkness encourages crime. Last month, there was the terrible mugging at the gates of the park. Now, old people are scared to go out after sunset and parents are unwilling to let children walk to Moseley youth club.

I realise that cuts in council expenditure have to be made but street-lighting should be protected. Surely the people of this town would be prepared to pay a little extra to turn the lights on again in Cotham. Then we will be free to walk our streets without fear.

Yours faithfully,
David Rumbold

■ *Exercise 15 Plan for a persuasive letter to a newspaper*

Above is a letter to a newspaper. Write out a plan Mr Rumbold might have used.

■ *Exercise 16 Informative letter to a newspaper*

Write a short, informative letter to a newspaper on one of the following topics:

a) You are holding a jumble sale for charity.
b) You are starting a football team to play in the local league.
c) You are starting a home for unwanted cats.

■ *Exercise 17 Persuasive letter to a newspaper*

Write one of the following letters. Make a simple plan beforehand.

a) A letter complaining about local facilities for young people.
b) A letter making a case for a nursery school.
c) A letter demanding noise restrictions at a local airport.
d) A letter objecting to dogs using a park near you.

Sometimes you respond to a letter in the paper. Perhaps your letter tries to disprove or contradict what you have read. The organisation of your response depends on what the first letter said. You must answer the main points. A response to Mr Rumbold's letter in Exercise 15 might have this plan:

> Lighting in Cotham no worse than in other parts of town. Pavements repaired annually – willing to deal with complaints Quote survey to show Cotham better than average for accidents Mugging took place at south side of Cotham Park – a different part of town
>
> End with sympathy for Mr Rumbold's ankle but not his argument.

■ *Exercise 18 Response to a letter in a newspaper*

Write a response to the letter you wrote for Exercise 17.

Response to an advertisement

A formal letter can be a response to an advertisement. You might, for example, want to buy something you have seen advertised. Here is a typical advertisement:

MINI **850** 1980 MOT, very clean, reliable, £1,200 o.n.o.
Apply Mr S Trent, 13, The Gables, TILBROOK.

If you are looking for a car, this advertisement might interest you. It does not give much information so the plan of your letter might be:

Indicate interest
Ask about mileage and colour
Can afford £1,100 only
Ask Mr Trent to ring

Resulting in:

37, Turnham Lane,
TILBROOK, ST5 9YT

8th August 1985

S Trent Esq.,
13, The Gables,
TILBROOK

Dear Mr Trent,

I saw your advertisement in today's Tilbrook Advertiser and I am interested in the Mini you have for sale.

You did not give the colour of the car or the mileage covered. I am not keen on white cars and I do not want a heavily-used vehicle.

The maximum I want to pay is £1,100 though I might manage a little more for a really good car. £1,200 does seem high for the year although you do state that you are open to offers.

Would you please ring me at Tilbrook 34267 after 6 pm.

Yours sincerely,
Dawn Johnson

■ *Exercise 19 Answering advertisements*

Reply to one of these advertisements:

a) Single woman wanted to share flat. Rent £20 per week – own room. Write to Jane Brogan, Melbury Towers, Harbour Road, BERWICK.

b) Collector buys old coins – any year, any condition. Send details of coins offered to Mr P Shawcliffe, 45, Brownsea Avenue, POOLE.

c) FOR SALE Top quality upholstery fabric, 1.5 metres wide, at the crazy price of £2 per metre. Available in Blue, Green, Red and Yellow. Send your order and money to Fine Fabrics Ltd, Manley Mill, BRADFORD.

Applying for a job

One of the most important types of formal letter is the job application. This gives your prospective employer a picture of you to convince him you are the right person for the job. When you make the plan, ask yourself:

What skills, qualifications and experience do I have for this job?

For some jobs all this information is put on a separate sheet called a *curriculum vitae*. In most cases, however, a letter on its own is sufficient. Look at this advertisement.

DRUMMOND HALL HOTEL AND RESTAURANT
have a vacancy for a
WEEKEND RECEPTIONIST
Saturday and Sunday 2 pm – 7 pm
Apply with details of experience to
The Manager,
Drummond Hall Hotel and Restaurant,
PEEBLES

How would you apply for this post? Well, clearly you would have to give details of experience. It might be useful to mention educational qualifications and clerical skills. It could be sensible, too, to explain why you want a part-time job with fairly unsocial hours. The plan might look like this:

I am applying for the advertised post
Details of previous experience in two hotels
Educational qualifications and clerical skills
Justification for applying
Sign off

and the finished letter might look like this:

37, Hawick Drive,
PEEBLES.

10th September 1987

The Manager,
Drummond Hall Hotel
and Restaurant,
PEEBLES

Dear Sir,
  I should like to apply for the post of weekend receptionist advertised in yesterday's Peebles Gazette.
  My last job, which I left in June 1985 to have a baby, was receptionist at the Edinburgh Rock Hotel. I was there for five years and, before that, I worked as a secretary/receptionist at the Roxburgh in Perth. The managers at both places are prepared to provide references.
  I left school in 1974 with 6 'O' Level passes to go to Secretarial College in Newcastle. My shorthand and typing are still fast and accurate. I found these skills very useful in my previous posts.
  My daughter is now three years old and I feel happy leaving her for short periods. I do not want a full-time job yet but I would enjoy working a few hours at weekends when my husband is at home to baby-sit.

Yours faithfully,
Anne Hyde

■ *Exercise 20 Job application letter*

Write an application letter responding to one of these advertisements:

a) Mechanic wanted for garage. Must be qualified and experienced. Apply to Manager, Thornton's Garage, MORPETH.
b) Laboratory Assistants required. Must be educated to '0' Level standard and be systematic in their approach to work. No experience needed as training will be given. Apply to Personnel Manager, Bio-Lab, STEVENAGE.
c) Personal Secretary wanted from 1st April for Director of small company making children's clothes. Write giving qualifications and experience to Mr L Butler, Lenbut Ltd, 45–49, Trafford Road, MANCHESTER 8.

Business letters

The most formal letter you are likely to write is not really from you at all but written on behalf of a firm or organisation. Business letters are hard to write and, often, even harder to read. They demand clear, simple writing and that means clear thinking before you write. Why are you writing? Are you –

informing?
explaining?
persuading?

Think about the reader as well. Ask yourself:

1 How much does the reader know already?
2 What is the reader's attitude to the subject of the letter?
3 How will the reader react to the letter?

You may not know the answers but you can make sensible guesses. Do not use complicated language in business letters. The rule is:

Use simple language wherever possible

help	*not*	assist
buy	*not*	purchase
make easier	*not*	facilitate
what we need	*not*	our requirements

Keep sentences short. A reader will lose track if sentences ramble.

Here is an example of a good business letter. It is direct and to the point.

Pressure Plastics,
37–41 Union Street,
SHEFFIELD,
SH2 3QT

13th June 1985

Lyraght and Watson,
14 Knox Street,
EDINBURGH.

Dear Mrs Lyraght,
   Thank you for your letter of 9th June. I am very please that the last batch of garden chairs got to you on time and that you sold them so quickly.
   We can certainly send you another 200 chairs by the end of June. You did not specify a colour so I will give you the same mixture as last time. If that is not what you want, please ring me.
   We no longer make the X21 table but I am enclosing a brochure for our new X23 table. It might suit you. It is a little dearer than the X21 but we think it is a much better piece of furniture. If you ring me quickly, you could have fifty X23 tables delivered with the chairs.

Yours sincerely,
John White
Sales Manager
Enc.

■ Exercise 21 Business letters

Write one of the following business letters:

a) to a supermarket publicising a new dessert your firm has produced.
b) to a company asking for payment of a bill outstanding for 10 months.
c) to the factory manager emphasising the importance of hygiene.

4 Words: using the right words

Formality and informality

Here are two descriptions of the same event:

I met my good friend Augustus.
I bumped into my old mate Gus.

The first description is straightforward but the second is more informal. The opposite effect can be achieved by using more formal language:

I encountered an intimate acquaintance of mine, one Mr Augustus Peabody.

Longer words are used and the "intimate acquaintance" gets his *full* name.

■ *Exercise 22 More formal – less formal*

Here are six sentences. Make the first three *more* formal and the second three *less* formal by changing the language.

a) I put my foot down and the old bus fairly flew along.
b) The fellow you were chatting with is a right crook.
c) He was the queerest old codger I had ever set eyes on.
d) We are compelled to make massive reductions in expenditure.
e) The climatic conditions have been particularly intemperate.
f) The police arrested the criminal.

■ *Exercise 23 Formal and informal words*

Divide the following list of words into *formal, informal* and *in-between*:

bash, beverage, booze, car, child, chilly, constabulary, crazy, digs, drink, considerable, excessively, intoxication, ordinary, police, rectify, repair, television, telly, toddle, transportation, tummy, walk.

Sometimes a piece of writing goes wrong because it is too formal or too informal. Look at this speech by the bride's father to be delivered at the reception:

Ladies and gentlemen, boys and girls, it is the responsibility of the bride's male parent to deliver an address at the conclusion of the meal. It gives me considerable pleasure to fulfil this function, to bid farewell to my beloved daughter and her chosen partner as they sail off together on the stormy oceans of life. It seems but yesterday that she was a tiny infant, nestled in the protective arms of her mother.

The guests would soon be snoring. The language does not fit the occasion. Here is a version which says the same things more simply:

Well everybody, I know you're waiting for me to make my speech. I hope you enjoyed the meal. Anyway, I want to wish all the best to the young couple. I am sure you'll do well together. Look after her, Mike, she's a good girl. Do you know it doesn't seem that long ago she was a baby. That shows how old I am, doesn't it?

The writing is simpler and sounds more genuine. The father's feelings come through.

■ Exercise 24 Getting the tone right

Write one of the following. Make sure you get the right tone of formality or informality.

a) A letter to your boss asking for a rise.
b) A talk to a group of eleven-year-old children thanking them for a donation to a charity you organise.
c) A statement to a policeman as a witness to an assault.
d) A description of college life to a friend who might come to college.

Complicated words can give a reader great problems. Long, difficult words are not wrong but to keep ignoring the simple words is silly.

■ Exercise 25 Simple words for long words

Here is a list of 20 long words. Find simpler words of the same meaning.

manufactured, terminate, demonstrate, authorise, emancipate, countenance, merchandise, lubricate, estimate, atmosphere, transformation, residence, discontinue, approximately, motionless, commencement.

5 Spelling: -sc- and -cc-

Usually the sound of a word is a good guide to spelling. Sometimes, though, the sound can trick you. In the word "fascinate" the -sc- sounds like an -s- on its own. Here is a list of words like that. Try to remember how to spell them.

adole-**sc**-ent

a-**sc**-end

a-**sc**-ertain

de-**sc**-end

fa-**sc**-inate

mi-**sc**-ellaneous

su-**sc**-eptible

efferve-**sc**-ent

the sc- sound can come at the beginning of a word as well:

sc-ene

sc-ent

sc-eptre

sc-ience

The letter "c" is found doubled in some words like "accident". The -cc- sounds like -x- which does not help spelling. Here is a list of words with -cc- in them:

a-**cc**-elerate

a-**cc**-ept

a-**cc**-ess

a-**cc**-ent

a-**cc**-ident

e-**cc**-entric

su-**cc**-eed

su-**cc**-ession

su-**cc**-inct

va-**cc**-ine

Some of the words in these lists may be unfamiliar. Look them up in a dictionary so you know what they mean as well as how to spell them.

■ *Exercise 26 Spelling*

Complete these sentences using words from the above lists. *Check your spelling.*

a) The cow was ill and the vet injected a . . . .

b) He still has a strange . . . . . . though he has spoken English for years.

c) The cars were involved in a terrible . . . .

d) Will you . . . . . . this small gift?

e) Wait here while I . . . . . . the stairs.

f) There is no . . . . . . through this door.

6 Exercises for revision

Exercise 27 Letter based on a diary

Here are the entries in Mrs Mackay's diary for one week. Read them, then write her weekly letter to a friend who lives in another part of the country.

Sunday – slept too late and felt off all day. We are decorating the bedroom and everything smells of paint. I made a cake which tasted of paint.

Monday – busy at work so boss asked me to stay on. We finished the bedroom tonight. Wallpaper is fine but the paint is very bright!

Tuesday – popped in to see old Mrs Durant. She showed me a picture of herself as a young girl. She looked very pretty in old-fashioned clothes.

Wednesday – woke up with a rotten cold. Went into work but Mrs Cooper sent me home at ten. Bed after tea with a whisky and lemon.

Thursday – felt much better this morning so went back to work. It was sunny in the afternoon so I walked in the park. George [her husband] and I went to the pictures in the evening.

Friday – Helen [her daughter] rang this evening from London. She wants us to go down for a weekend. George is not keen but I said we would.

Saturday – bought an orange cardigan at market this morning. George went to the match in the afternoon and Jenny came in for a chat. In the evening George and I went to The Sun for a drink. Came home about eleven.

Exercise 28 Letter based on a diary

Write your diary for last week and use it as the basis for a letter to a friend.

Exercise 29 Commas

Cut out the unnecessary commas in the following passage:

The space ship, Survival, stood, on the tarmac, a huge silver cigar, pointed, like a dramatic finger, at the darkening,

November sky. Scaffolding reached, halfway up its sides, and, stopped, as though the builders had run out of materials, or been seized with a sudden, fear of heights. In the flight office, the chief, controller stared at her video-screen and, thought of tomorrow. Then, that giant bulk would spout flame, tear itself free, from the supporting derrick, and, lunge into space, shrugging off gravity, like a dog shakes off water. If, all went well, a new chapter, in space history would begin, and, the future of the world, would change from certain disaster, to a glimmering hope of salvation.

■ Exercise 30 Commas and semi-colons

Add commas and semi-colons where needed in this passage:

The interviewer a man of more years than his make-up admitted smiled shuffled his papers and then inclined his head as the next victim uneasy and vulnerable took her seat. She had been a film star but was now full of doubt her past assurance drained from her by years of popular rejection. She sat touching her face occasionally trying to revive a fading beauty and always hunched forward as though any loud noise would send her scurrying from the stage. He was not loud however his approach was quiet gentle almost feline. Without her realisation he would systematically expose her to *his* television audience as a self-doubting drug-dependent wreck. When the demolition process was over his smile would harden his hand dismiss her and the camera would swing back to him. She would be back in oblivion until another chat-show host felt like exhibiting her as a mildly interesting example of the has-been the vaguely familiar face.

■ Exercise 31 Commas, colons and semi-colons

Add commas, colons and semi-colons where needed in this passage:

The machine had gone berserk it was spewing out sausages of all shapes and dimensions. Huge round sausages minute square sausages elliptic sausages of medium size and specimens defying description churned out of the pipe at an incredible rate. It was impossible to switch off the machine it had jammed. Denis roared with laughter Mr Leslie was speechless with rage. Due to his own incompetence profits were being thrown away. Mr Leslie's temper needed someone to blame. The scapegoat was Denis the only available choice. Mr Leslie grasped a bloated sausage the largest representative of the machine's invention and began to beat Denis over the head. The boss's tennis club experience gave his blows variety forehand volleys backhand drives drop-shots and smashes. Denis fell to the floor giggling hysterically to be engulfed by an avalanche of misshapen bangers.

Exercise 32 Complaint letter

Write a complaint letter on one of the following topics:

a) A watch, bought seven months ago with a year's guarantee, will not go.
b) You bought six rose bushes by mail order. They have not flowered.
c) Your hair, washed and permed yesterday, has turned orange.

Exercise 33 Complaint letter

Read this passage. Then write the letter of complaint which Mrs Lloyd sent to the council.

Mrs Lloyd's council house was supposed to be decorated in 1982 but nobody came to do the job. Nothing happened in 1983 despite letters and phone calls. Eventually, Mrs Lloyd got permission over the phone to do the job herself as she was fed up with the faded paint and grubby wallpaper. She finished in June 1984. To her amazement, the week after, a team of men from the council arrived to decorate. She told them the job was done and they left. The next day, however, a letter came, signed by a Mr Cross, saying that her house *had* to be decorated in accordance with council rules even though she had done the job already *without council permission*. Mr Cross was prepared to overlook this breach of council rules but the workmen would be returning next month. Mrs Lloyd tried to phone Mr Cross several times without success and, in the end, she decided to write.

■ *Exercise 34 Letter to a newspaper*

Write a letter to your local newspaper publicising one of the following:

a) a new group to help local consumers
b) a new club for joggers
c) a sponsored event for charity (you choose the event and the charity)

■ *Exercise 35 Application letter*

Find an advertisement for a job and write two application letters. Invent experience and qualifications in the first; be completely honest in the second.

■ *Exercise 36 Business letter*

Write a business letter on one of the following topics:

a) Giving a quotation and delivery date for 100 pine tables.
b) Apologising to a customer for overcharging and enclosing a refund.
c) Arranging a weekend convention of sales staff at a hotel.

■ *Exercise 37 Spelling*

Correct the spelling in the following passage:

As I assended the stairs, I had a nasty axident. I tripped over a septre which had been left there and dessended very fast. After, I acertained that the culprit had been the hotel's lovable eggs-entric who spoke with a Rumanian aksent. Anyway, I suckseeded in breaking misselaneous bones and was taken to hospital in an ambulance that axcelerated through the traffic. I was a most irassible patient. It appears that I was suseptible to the cent of the vacxine they pumped into me. I was facinated by the sukcinct manner of the doctor who finally suxeeded in curing me. I was ackcepted back into the hotel and allowed axess to the lift in future.

UNIT FIVE

1 Essays: telling a story

A narrative essay tells a story. You must first consider:

the plot
the characters
the setting

Planning the plot

1 Check that the title says *exactly* what you think it does. Don't write a marvellous essay on "The Misfit" and when your time is up, discover that the title is "Misfits".

2 Keep your basic plan *very* simple.
Surprise and tension come later, from the characters, from descriptions, and above all from the way you handle language.

3 *Never* begin too far from the main event. For example, do *not* begin "The Fight" by explaining:
how you got a ticket for the football match;
how you got a day off to go;
how the match went;
how you were separated from your friends.
or "The Fight" might not have time to start.

4 Aim at about FIVE paragraphs, with one main point in each – and make the main event begin not later than the second or third paragraph. One very useful pattern is this one:

SAMPLE TITLE: **The storm**
PARAGRAPH 1 Place and time   *Grimsby, fishing trawler, winter*
PARAGRAPH 2 People involved   *2 sailors who hate each other*
PARAGRAPH 3 Begin main event *bad weather – gets worse*
PARAGRAPH 4 The crisis   *abandon ship, 2 enemies save each other*
PARAGRAPH 5 Crisis over   *2 men become friends*

Planning the characters

1 *Never* include too many characters: two or three are usually as many as you can cope with properly in 500 words.

2 Plan what each one is like and will do.
Notice how short stories and plays concentrate on *one* main situation, involving only a few characters, at one particular time in their lives.

3 Avoid writing as if you are a child, an animal or anyone who uses very simple language or a lot of slang.

Planning the setting

1 Give your essay a special setting, with interesting things happening. For example:
Plot: a murder story
Setting: Wimbledon during the finals of the Women's Singles
                Westminister Abbey during a royal wedding
                Cambridge during a Real Ale Festival

Use something you know about – from carnival time in Trinidad to GCE examinations at college.

2 Choose a time of year to suit your plot – and refer to it throughout the story, linking the season with the events to give them extra significance.

3 The flashback technique is a good way of using time to give your story a framework. For example:
Paragraph 1 in the present, introducing one or two characters – perhaps someone now rich and famous.
Paragraph 2 remembers the past – the same man or woman twenty years ago, struggling with poverty – perhaps nicer.
Paragraphs 3 and 4 – the story of his or her success.
Paragraph 5 returns to the present, to the situation described in paragraph one.

Thinking of ideas

If you look at your essay title and you cannot think of anything to say, remember that there is *never* just one perfect way of writing about any title. *All you need is a situation. The whole story can grow from that.*

1 Use your *own* experience to help you with characters, incidents or background information.

2 *Use books, newspapers and television for ideas.* Research topics thoroughly. You can learn how to climb Everest or be a star, with some imagination.

3 Take *one* incident which seems to fit the mood of the title: a bank robbery, a divorce, an old person driving the wrong way up a one-way street. Then work out Reasons and Results and the story is as good as written. There are many alternatives for any one title. For example:

The Motorbike

Plan 1   Boy works hard for two years, saves to buy a motorbike. Buys it. Killed riding it for the first time.

Plan 2   Widow, 50. Only child, son, wants a motorbike – she won't allow it. Rows, resentment. He suddenly decides he wants a car instead (invent reason). Both happy again.

Plan 3   Boy wants a new motorbike – will never have the money: friends laugh at his old scooter. Steals bike from car park – excitement, joy – then fear. Abandons it, arrested, loses job and girlfriend.

Plan 4   Motorbike factory closes down, workers sit in – then take over, get backers, win orders, factory saved.

Plan 5   Firm offers prize: new bike plus £1,000 to Worker of the Year, elected by fellow workers.
Three favourites, one tells the story.
Things go wrong at crucial stage – sabotage?
Feelings when he wins/doesn't win.

Making your story interesting

Once story, setting and characters are decided, you have two main aims:

1 to make the story clear and easy to understand
2 to make it interesting by every means you can think of.

1 Each story must have *one main crisis* or it will seem pointless.

Include minor crises too – things which could be crucial, but turn out not to be. For example:
  Girl drives home, late at night, alone
  Remembers row with boyfriend (minor crisis)
  Car breaks down on lonely road (minor crisis)
  Leaves car, walks
  Hears footsteps, terrified (minor crisis)
  Only a man walking his dog
  Recovers, reaches home, looks for key
  Hand covers her mouth, from behind (main crisis)
  Knife blade flashes
Warning: If you use more than two or three surprises, the reader will start to *expect* the unexpected and the effect will be lost.

2 *Contrast the moods* in your story. For example, begin horror and murder stories with normal, pleasant people and situations.

3 *Contrast the pace* of events. Exciting parts must move faster, so use *short* words, *short* sentences and one or two *short* paragraphs. For example:
"Quick! Help! There's a fire!"
  Just before a crisis, slow down the story. Use description and *longer* sentences to emphasise the lack of action. Then the crisis will seem more vivid by contrast.

■ *Exercise 1 First person narration*

Write an essay on ONE of the following titles in which one of the characters tells the story in the first person.

a) The Merger   c) The Power Cut
b) D Day   d) Diamonds Are Not For Ever

■ *Exercise 2 Adapting plots*

a) Read *two* short stories from any collection of short stories.
b) Summarise each one in about 100 words.
c) Use one of the summaries as the basis of a story of your own. Provide your own title.

■ *Exercise 3 Special setting and narrative essay*

a) Plan the events of a murder story *and* the characters involved.
b) Make brief notes on a special event you could use as a background to the story: anything from a space rocket launch to a tiddlywinks contest.
c) Write the murder story, then provide *three* alternative titles for it.

■ *Exercise 4 Flashback technique*

Write on one of the following titles using the flashback technique *and* a time of year which suits the mood of your story.

a) Hard Times
b) The Day I Put My Foot Down
c) The Last Conference
d) The Breakdown

■ *Exercise 5 Alternative plots and narrative essay*

a) Choose ONE of the following titles and write a brief outline of *five* different stories you could use in writing the essay.

Moving House
The Marriage Ends
The Pools Winner
The Shoplifters

b) Using *one* of the outlines you have written, write a more detailed plan, then the essay.

■ *Exercise 6 Including several crises*

Write a plan for ONE of the following titles indicating where the main crisis and *two* other minor crises should occur. Then write the essay.

a) The First Prize
b) Any Tom, Dick or Harry
c) The Rubbish Dump
d) The Treasure

Newspaper stories

Some newspapers use more complicated words and sentences than others, which have smaller pages and more pictures. Generally, the following rules will help you to write a newspaper story which seems like the real thing.

1 Use a dramatic main heading: this will be short, in note form and often use words beginning with the same letter. Try to catch attention, *not* explain what happened. For example:

<u>M</u>AD <u>M</u>ICK IN <u>M</u>URDER <u>M</u>YSTERY!

2 Use short paragraphs, and brief headings to give a taste of what the next few lines are about.

> **LOCAL WOMAN IN EVEREST BID**
>
> When 30-year-old Cliff Hanger leads a 10-man British team up Everest next month, attractive, red-haired Judy Denmark will be one of the "men".
>
> Judy, a 21-year-old ski instructor, is staying at her parents' house in Park Crescent until she leaves for Nepal on Friday.
>
> *Loves Heights*
>
> "Heights? I just love them," Judy told reporters yesterday . . . .

3 Use brief, but exaggerated language. Leave out all spare words for example, "the" often disappears from the beginning of sentences, and numbers appear in figures, not in words:

> **Local councillors were last night in uproar**
> **after rumours of near bankruptcy and**
> **huge rate increases.**
>
> Trouble began when work was held up on the ring road and costs jumped to a staggering £17 million within a year. January's ice and snow added a massive £20 million to the road clearing bill alone and over 1,000 families had to be re-housed when council houses were flooded in the thaw.

Simple language saves space, is easier to understand and gives a faster, more dramatic pace, aided by the exaggerations.

Use in uproar	*not* in disagreement
Use massive	*not* very large
Use starving	*not* suffering from vitamin deficiency
Use shock death	*not* unexpected demise

4 Begin with a reference to a time – or a day if you are thinking of a weekly paper, not a daily one.

> **Late last night** police investigating the latest Red Terror murder in Glasgow swooped on the Park West flats near Putnoe.

Straightaway this makes the story seem more definite, factual and up-to-date.

5 Refer to everyone involved, from experts to eye witnesses. Then add realism and drama by quoting brief statements from several of them, giving briefly all the facts you can fit in, even some only indirectly connected with the main event. For example:

> Blonde, blue-eyed Mrs Betty Jeans, 32-year-old mother of twins said tearfully, "We had only just gone into the store when there was a terrible bang, and everyone started screaming.
>
> "We were lucky, we were near the door, but people further in were trapped when the ceiling fell down. I shall never forget it, never."

6 These people would still be mentioned, even if reporters failed to interview them: and some scrap of "human interest" would be added if possible.

7 Refer to a photograph which accompanies your article, but – of course – never waste time drawing one! Simply leave a space for it and write a *brief* caption underneath it.

■ *Exercise 7 Newspaper article*

Write a front page story for your local weekly paper on one of the following:

a) a fire in a large department store
b) a raid on a local bank
c) a local couple winning a fortune on the football pools
d) a strike at a local factory and violence at the picket lines

2 Language: punctuating conversation

Direct speech

When you write down exactly what someone has said you are writing Direct Speech. Your sentence will fall into two parts:

a) the *exact* words which were said aloud;
b) "identification" words to explain who was talking and how it was said.

Inside your own written sentence, then, is another one – the speaker's.

"**I've dropped my icecream!**" said the little girl crossly as someone yelled in the stalls below.

1 Only the actual words spoken aloud go between the inverted commas (which curve towards the speech rather like the tops of a pair of brackets).

2 Use single inverted commas *or* the more traditional double ones but stick to the ones you choose for *all* the speech you quote, whoever says it. Don't use single commas for some speakers, double commas for others.

3 If you are not sure which words to put between the inverted commas, try underlining those you *think* are the actual words spoken, in pencil, to make them stand out from the others. Would the underlined words sound right if they were said aloud *exactly* as they are? For example:

RIGHT: I told him, "**I only want to borrow a pound.**"
WRONG: I told him "**that I only wanted to borrow a pound.**"

■ *Exercise 8 Direct speech*

Put inverted commas around the Direct Speech in the following sentences.

a) Thanks to the snow we all have a suntan said the manager of the football team.
b) That sounds odd said the reporter.

c) We couldn't play here so we went to Tunisia for a month to train he explained.

d) We're hoping for more snow soon he added hopefully.

Punctuating direct speech

1 The speaker's sentence *must* begin with a capital letter, even when it is not the first word in your own written sentence.

 The assistant said happily, "That's the nicest customer I've served for a long time."

2 If a sentence starts with identification words (*The assistant said happily*) use a comma before the inserted commas open.

3 The speaker's sentence *must* end with some punctuation mark *before* you close the inverted commas on it.

 "Come here!" the assistant shouted.
 "Why should I?" she demanded.
 "If you don't ..." he glared at her.
 "Please dear, I think -" began her husband.
 "That's the rudest man I've ever met," she fumed.

4 If your written sentence goes on *after* the speaker's sentence ends, *his* has no full stop and *yours* continues with a *small* letter, not a capital.

 RIGHT: "But he thinks you've stolen his sausages!" said her husband.

 WRONG: "What sausages?" She asked.

 WORSE: "The ones that have fallen into your umbrella" He said, laughing.

 In the last example the words "he said" explain who was talking, so they belong to the *same* written sentence as the quoted speech, and must use a small -h, not a capital.

5 If somebody's speech is interrupted in mid-sentence, there is *no* need for a capital letter to begin the second part of his sentence, and a question or exclamation mark doesn't come until his sentence ends:

 "I don't think –" his friend turned even paler at the sound of gunfire nearby, "– that we're safe anywhere!"

6 But if two spoken sentences are just separated by identification words, you do begin the second one with a *capital* letter.

"It's hard if your parents are immigrants," he said, thoughtfully. "You don't know which side you're on."

■ *Exercise 9   Inverted commas and commas*

Insert capital letters, inverted commas and other punctuation marks needed in the following sentences:

a) The ringmaster announced there will be a short interval while the deputy lion tamer prepares to take over.
b) Just a minute she called you've forgotten your change.
c) Do you mean to tell me he demanded that you've given my best pullover to the scouts' jumble sale.
d) That'll be the day he laughed scornfully that'll be the day when you get up early without being nagged.
e) He looked doubtful then said quietly if you're really sure he hesitated again about selling the car I mean then we could manage the bigger mortgage.

Making it clear who said it

1 When people are talking, each person's speech needs:
Either   a new *line* starting against the margin, if the sentence begins with identification words;
Or   a new paragraph, starting away from the margin if the sentence begins with Direct Speech.
For example:

> "He can't do anything so stupid. He's got so much to be thankful for," the younger man exclaimed.
> "So have thousands of men who suddenly throw everything up and disappear into thin air," the older man replied.
> Jake, the younger man, looked desperate. "He's my father! He can't just disappear. He can't!"

Notice that each fresh comment had a new paragraph *except* the last one, "He's my father . . ." because that followed description of the speaker, Jake.

2 When two or more speakers are involved, especially when they are of the same sex, make it clear who is speaking. Do not put names in brackets – re-phrase the sentence.

WRONG: He (Jake) didn't dare look up for a while. "But surely –" he began.
"No buts!" he (Roy) replied, sternly.

RIGHT: Jake didn't dare look up for a while.
"But surely –" he began.
"No buts!" the other man replied sternly.

3 If a speaker quotes somebody else, or mentions the title of a book, film or play, and you are already using double inverted commas, use single ones for the newly quoted material. (Alternatively, titles can simply be underlined.)

"Have you seen that new musical 'Catch a Falling Starlet'?"
"Yes I saw it last month," he said. "I thought it was good too. But I still haven't seen 'The Rodent Trap', have you?"

■ Exercise 10 Punctuating conversation

Punctuate the following passage and use capital letters, new lines and new paragraphs wherever they are needed.

Television is a curse she burst out infuriated you used to come home and talk to me now you just press different buttons on the box until you fall asleep in your chair you enjoy television as much as I do what happens on Tuesdays he said as she began to deny it when the Kung Fu serial's on there's no chance of seeing anything else then there's the late night chat show the horror movie that's not fair she exclaimed going a sort of magenta colour rather like the Channel 3 newsreader's velvet jacket if you won't talk to me what is there to do but watch television do you mean to say he interrupted that if I promised to talk to you you wouldn't watch television for a week I don't believe it what do you bet she said a fiver it's not enough I bet you that I can go without television and here she threw the *Radio Times* dramatically into the rubbish bucket for two weeks and if I manage it we'll send the set back he turned pale.

Indirect speech

Quoted speech, in inverted commas, is called Direct Speech. If you record what someone has said without using inverted commas, this is called *Indirect* or *Reported speech*.

Direct Speech	*Indirect or Reported Speech*
uses PRESENT tense	uses PAST tense (or time)
NEEDS inverted commas	needs NO inverted commas
CALLS the speaker "I"	NAMES the speaker
CALLS the listener "You"	NAMES the listener
REPEATS the actual words spoken	CHANGES the spoken words
HAS NO link word to join what was said and who said it	NEEDS a link word to join what was said and who said it (e.g. that/to/whether)

For example:

Direct Speech	*Indirect Speech or Reported Speech*
"*Go back, you'll fall*"	Courene told him *to go back or he would fall.*
"*Can you direct me* to the police station please?"	She asked *whether the man could direct her to the police station.*

If you have to change Direct Speech into Reported or Indirect Speech and it is not clear whether a speaker was male or female, assume it was male *or* use a description such as "the speaker" or "the enquirer".

■ *Exercise 11 Indirect or Reported Speech*

Re-write Exercises 9 and 10 in indirect or reported speech.

3 Essays: writing a dialogue

Dialogues are very difficult to do well, so avoid choosing a dialogue in an essay examination, if you can.

If you have no alternative, remember that a dialogue essay must have a beginning, a middle and end, like any other essay.

1 *Plan the characters:* decide *exactly* how they would behave and the things they would care about. Decide:

how old they are

the kind of house, furniture, neighbours they have

what they look like

how they get on together normally

how they talk

how they spend their money – how they *would* spend it, if they had more

whether there are others in the family who would make awkward situations even worse

2 *Plan the events.* Decide what happened before, during *and* after the central conversation.

3 *Follow the general advice* on narrative essays. Remember there should be minor crises as well as one major one.

4 *Build in reasons for conflict* to make the conversation interesting. Make the people contrast with each other, give them opposing views. Give them faults too.

5 *Refer to the past.* Make people mention ordinary things about their daily life, like forgetting to buy toothpaste or arguing with the neighbours about the fence.

6 *Let facts emerge through what people say.*

WRONG: Mr Jayson sat, exhausted, in the chair.
He worked in the china department of a big store and, now the January sales were on, he had to stand for eight hours a day, serving hot, bad-tempered customers.

BETTER: John sat slumped in the chair.
"Tea love?"
He stirred, forcing his eyes to focus on his wife.
"I don't know – no, yes, all right, thanks. Oh!"
He tried to reach up to take the cup. "My back!"
"Oh Jane it was terrible today. We didn't have a break till half past one and then the queue was so long in the canteen I only had five minutes to sit down.
"I'll go mad if I have another day like today – those people were fighting each other for bits of chipped china, just because there was ten pence off!"

Some facts have to be given as "author's comments" to save time, but the things which affect characters most are the ones they need to talk about, as real people do.

7 *Use other people*
Facts can, however, take far too long to explain in speech; also John would not tell his wife:

"I'm so tired because I work in the china department of a big store and the January sales are on."

She already knows that. Bring in a Sympathetic Stranger, then you can give a lot of information quickly, believably and without "author comment". Do this early in the essay, when the reader needs information.
Use an old friend being given up-to-date news, a family doctor, someone at work or in the bus queue, but make the episode brief because it has to be a short cut to information.

8 *Use identification words* (he said/she replied) carefully. When you do include them, vary them:

do not always use "said".
do not always put quoted words first and "identification words" second (or vice versa).

9 *Include some brief description* from time to time, to give a change from the conversation, *though about two thirds of a dialogue essay ought to be made up of speech.*

Play scripts

Always set out dialogue in the way already described, unless the instructions say clearly you can use "any way you wish" or "the style of a play script".

If the play script method *is* allowed, the layout is very simple:

1 describe the scene, briefly, at the beginning in the *present* tense;
2 write the name of the speaker in the margin on the left, at the beginning of *every* speech;
3 write the *exact* words spoken by the side of each speaker's name, never in the margin;
4 use *no* inverted commas;
5 use *no* identification words, such as "she cried" or "he shouted";
6 "stage instructions" should be very brief, written in brackets and use the present tense.

Mr Drummond is vacuum cleaning as the door bursts open.

Courene (rushing in)*:* Dad, I've got it! I've got it!

Mr Drummond: Stop squashing me like that girl! Stop it, you'll break the vacuum cleaner! Now then, what is it you've got?

Courene (crazy with excitement)*:* The job! I've got that job. They liked my photographs and I'm going to New York!

(She drags her father into a quick bout of discotheque athletics.)

■ *Exercise 12 Dialogue*

Re-write the last example, setting it out as ordinary conversation instead of as a play script. Add identification words whenever necessary, but do not change the Direct Speech.

■ *Exercise 13 Play script*

Write a conversation between three students who are stuck in the college lift after an evening class. Aim at using 450–500 words.

■ *Exercise 14 Dialogue*

An elderly couple has just had a letter from the local authority telling them the street where they live is to be demolished. They are to be re-housed in a council flat and can inspect the three alternatives straight away. Write their conversation.

4 Words: saying it more powerfully

First, decide what *kind* of writing you are being asked to do.

Relaxed and informal – for direct speech or a friendly letter
Formal and precise – for a report or a business letter
Dramatic and imaginative – for narrative or descriptive writing

Then try to use the kind of words *and* way of putting them together that suit the style.

Imaginative writing

Choosing the right words

1 Use words which sound like what they describe:

> your head *thumps, pounds* or *throbs* when it aches
> a tree *rustles, groans* or *cracks* in a gale.

2 Words can do more than simply imitate sounds. Try choosing words which sound like the MOOD you are using: harsh-sounding words to show anger; slick, efficient ones to be business-like; gentle ones to talk about sorrow, sickness or love. For example, both of the following sentences describe curtains, but rather different ones:

Great loops of soft, shining silk shimmered in the moonlight.
A wodge of rough sacking was shoved across the gap.

To sound alert, or violent, use "harsh" consonants such as:
b ch g t c d k z
For example:

alert	business	chuck	guts
bank	contract	chisel	scratch
barter	deposit	gouge	splinter

To sound soft, weird, quiet or sleepy, use long vowel sounds, like -oo and -ah, and soft consonants such as:
f l n w h m sh y

For example:

fainting	lulling	mourn	soothe
feel	melt	shade	whisper
heal	moon	shimmer	willow

Words ending in -ing and -ly often have this soft effect.

3 Instead of using different letters to give the mood you want, repeat the *same* consonant several times. This is called ALLITERATION. Repeating a vowel is called ASSONANCE.

> *soft -w, -s and -i sounds:*
> The winds whispered to the sobbing girl, sighing wistfully that Simon had lied.
>
> *harder -s, -t and -d:*
> The sabres struck and slashed, strong steel flashed in the sun and the stones were soaked in blood.
>
> *or -b, for vitality:*
> She was bubbling with glee, absolutely bursting to break the news: she'd been and beaten the lot of them!

> *Warning:* Do not repeat the same letter too often.
> Do not use it always at the beginning of words.

■ *Exercise 15 Choosing for sound*

a) Arrange the following words in two groups, one for those which sound soft, the other for the harder sounds.

b) Use each word in a sentence, concentrating carefully on choosing a mood *and* other words which match it.

strike	smash	spit	floating	shell	stutter
eerie	lake	gouge	wish	zip	velvet
gestapo	smooth	pitch	fist	screech	grab

■ *Exercise 16 Choosing for sound*

Using about 150 words, write a description of ONE of the following. Choose words which match the sounds and feelings involved.

a) The scene before, during and after a thunderstorm.

b) Sitting in a dentist's chair and having a tooth filled.

c) A junior school playground before, during and after playtime.

■ *Exercise 17 Alliteration*

Write an advertising slogan, using obvious alliteration, for EACH of the following:

a) a car
b) pet food
c) a cure for headaches *or* for spots and pimples
d) a new magazine

Choosing vivid comparisons

Try comparing what you are writing about with something *unexpected* using a SIMILE or a METAPHOR.

Not	He's rather dull.	*but*	He's *as interesting as a bowl of cold tripe.* (Simile)
Not	The learner driver was very nervous.	*but*	The learner driver was *as nervous as a knife-thrower's assistant whose boss has just lost his glasses.* (Simile)

The comparisons used so far are similes – which say that one thing is *similar* to, *like* or *as* another. A metaphor would say that one actually *was* the other.
For example:

Similes
The man was AS ugly AS a toad.
The politician's tactics are SIMILAR to those of a head-hunting cannibal.

Metaphors
The man WAS a toad.
That politician IS a head-hunting cannibal.

First choose the characteristic you want to stress. Then think of something very different which also has that characteristic.
On the blueness of the sky:

blue paint	– could be useful
a hedge sparrow's eggs	– could be useful
blue eyeshadow	– could be useful
blue sea	– used too often already
blue cornflowers	– used too often already
blue jokes	– useful if the description *is not* to be taken seriously

■ *Exercise 18 Similes and metaphors*

Which of the following are similes, which are metaphors, and which are straightforward descriptions?

a) She's as lazy as a tourist with sunstroke.
b) She's idle, just like her sister.
c) He's got as much initiative as a puppet that's lost its strings.
d) He's as good at running this company as the lift boy would be.
e) It's as easy for a camel to enter the eye of a needle as it is to find a job in Solihull.
f) Put an ordinary lad into supporter's colours on a football train and you turn him into a walking hand grenade.
g) His puffy face had such a pale suntan he looked rather like a chocolate mousse.
h) He had a chocolate mousse of a face – puffy and slightly tanned.

■ *Exercise 19 Similes and metaphors*

Write a description of ONE of the following in about 150 words and include *at least* one simile and one metaphor.

a) The room you are in
b) An empty football ground
c) A derelict house or factory
d) An airport building

Using vivid descriptions

Description is needed, even when you are concentrating on telling a story. Once the situation in your essay is clear, stop the story for a few lines to describe how it feels to be a character involved in it.

1 Never try to include *too many* details at once. Avoid choosing the most obvious things.

2 Use all five senses if you can. Use hearing, taste, smell and touch, as well as sight, to make the reader live through the experience.

3 Long descriptions do hold up the action, so use them before and after a crisis as a *contrast*.

■ *Exercise 20 Using all your senses*

Write on at least ONE of the following situations using roughly 150 words to describe how it feels.

a) Someone has just had a really good meal which he enjoyed, but he has eaten far too much. He feels increasingly unwell.

b) Someone wakes up in the middle of the night feeling cold and clutching an icy hot water bottle. She lies there feeling more and more miserable but doesn't want to get up to fetch another blanket.

c) You have been running too fast, too long and with your mouth open. You have to stop running and sit down to recover. The pain in your chest is frightful.

d) It's the end of a tiring day and your new shoes have been hurting for hours. Now the pain is unbearable. You take them off, then have to put them on again and walk to the bus stop. You feel the blisters rubbing.

e) You are fast asleep when the alarm clock wakes you at 6 am. It is pitch black and bitterly cold but you have to leave the warm bed to get ready for work. You force yourself to stay awake and get up.

■ *Exercise 21 Using all the senses*

Choose a photograph from a newspaper or magazine.

a) Write roughly 150 words describing how *one* of the characters feels.

b) Continue the essay as a narrative, explaining how the character came to be in this situation and what happened afterwards.

5 Spelling: -i before -e (and exceptions)

The best known spelling rule in English is bound to be:
-i before **-e** EXCEPT after **c**. *For example:*

ceiling	conceited	deceive	receive
conceit	conceivably	perceive	receipt

-ei- exceptions

1 Sometimes you add re- to a word beginning with -i:
For example: re-introduce, re-iterate

2 – or you add -ing to one of the few words which still have to keep their final -e.
For example: be + ing, see + ing
Normally, of course, the -e disappears from the end of a word before -ing is added on:

make + ing = making   bake + ing=baking
take + ing = taking   rake + ing=raking

3 Other EI words just have to be learned by heart.

Common exceptions		*Less common*
beige		*exceptions*
eiderdown	rein (+ reindeer)	albeit
eight (+ eighteen)	seize (+ seizure)	caffeine
either (+ neither)	veil	deign
height (+ heighten)	vein	deity
heir (+ heiress)	weigh (+ weight)	feint
leisure		geiger
neighbour		geisha
reign		heifer
		heinous

■ *Exercise 22 ei without -c*

a) Use TEN of the common ei words, listed above, in separate sentences, to show their meaning. For example:

We wanted a *beige* carpet, but the local shops had only cream or brown and no shades in between.

Then write a sentence for each of the less common ei words.

6 Exercises for revision

■ *Exercise 23 Narrative essay*

a) Write a *brief* outline of FIVE different stories you could write about the photograph on the front page of any newspaper. Invent a suitable title for each one.
b) Write a more thorough plan for *one* of the five:
     include a special background event or situation;
     describe the main characters;
     indicate where the main crisis *and* two minor ones occur.
c) Write the essay in about 500 words. Aim at doing the whole of this exercise in *one and a quarter* hours.

■ *Exercise 24 Flashback technique*

Write one of the following stories, beginning and ending in the present but remembering past events for the main part of the story. *Remember* Do NOT mix past and present in the same paragraph

a) The Black Sheep
b) Rags and Riches
c) The Immigrant
d) The Celebrity

■ *Exercise 25 First person narrative*

Write on ONE of the following titles, making one character tell the story in the first person. Write about 500 words and take one hour to plan and write the essay.

a) The Breaker
b) Old Joe
c) The Ugly Duckling
d) Snakes and Ladders

■ *Exercise 26 Direct and reported speech*

a) Add capital letters, inverted commas and all other punctuation necessary for the following:

> Mum I want to leave college said Karen blurting it out quickly before she lost her nerve but you've still got two terms before your exams said her mother I don't want to take the exams Karen said going bright red I want to leave and get a job but said her mother you've already done a year at college and I know the girl butted in but I hate it I didn't want to do it in the first place but you and Dad insisted that's not fair her mother replied beginning to get angry we did want you to go to college but you didn't have any other ideas I know I'm sorry Karen began to cry I didn't mind it last year but now there are the exams coming and there are tests and I know I'm going to fail she gave up trying to explain put her head in her hands and began to sob in great shuddering gasps.

b) Re-write the passage in Reported Speech.

■ *Exercise 27 Choosing for sound*

Write a description of a lively party, choosing words which sound lively and cheerful. Include several examples of alliteration and assonance and write about 500 words.

■ *Exercise 28 Similes and metaphors*

Write a description of TWO of the following, using similes and metaphors to make your descriptions more vivid and underlining each one you include. Try to involve all five senses also. Write about 200 words for each description.

a) A journey in a hot, crowded train
b) Queuing for a bus, in the rush hour, in the rain
c) A walk in the country
d) A football match
e) A stock car or greyhound race

■ *Exercise 29 ie or ei*

Fill the blanks in the following sentences with -ie or -ei.

a) I perc--ved that the conc--ted man looked at me as though I were a th--f. Fortunately I had a rec--pt for the b--ge --derdown, alb--t a rather crumpled one. Afterwards I mentioned I "sp--d" for a BBC consumer group and he then tr--d to be fr--ndly!

b) My new n--ghbour seems to have plenty of l--sure: no canned beans and frozen french fr--s for her but home-made soups and p--s, or so she says.
Of course, her oven is brand new: mine looks like an h--rloom.

e) She always l--s about her w--ght! She's not under --ght stone and never will be if she doesn't give up the l--surely life: it nearly gives her a s--zure to walk to work – and she only walks from the car park!

d) He tr--d to s--ze my bag but it was t--d to my bicycle and when I cr--d for help my fr--nd grabbed him. He's been sentenced to do community service, but only --ghteen hours which is far too br--f if you ask me.

UNIT SIX

1 Comprehension: multiple choice exercises

Multiple choice questions are accompanied by several possible answers. Only one of them is the right one.

Question: An anchorite is which of the following?
A   A semi-precious metal
B   A religious recluse
C   Someone who likes a certain brand of butter
D   A sailor responsible for dropping a ship's anchor
E   The block from which an anchor is suspended
Answer: B

As in all comprehension exercises, you have to:
1 understand the information given to you;
2 decide what the questions are asking for;
3 choose the facts most closely related to each question.
You then copy down the number or letter (or both) which indicates each answer you choose.
Remember: You do not write out the answer in your own words.
            You do not give reasons for your choice.

Choosing the right one

There are usually *five* possible answers per question:

one may trap you with a word similar to the right one *or* like one in the question.
two are often partly true – *but also contain something untrue*.
one is the dangerous "distractor" – because it sounds so sensible.
Look for the answer which combines a fact from the passage *with a logical deduction*. Then reject it.
One will be completely correct.

For example:

Information: Jack and Jill fell down the hilly street.

Question: What happened in this street accident?

Possible answers:

A   Jill sat on a tuffet eating curds and whey.

B   Jack twisted his ankle and fell over.

C   Jill fell down the hill and was very upset.

D   Jill went for a walk with Jack.

E   Jack fell down.

Analysis

A   *Jill sat on a tuffet eating curds and whey.* A muddled nursery rhyme – obviously wrong.

B   *Jack twisted his ankle and fell over.* Jack did fall over – but we know nothing about the ankle-twisting, so do not choose this one.

C   *Jill fell down on the hill and was very upset.* Now the first part is true – but the second, about being upset, is only a deduction. What if Jack and Jill were just messing about? They could have fallen over – then just giggled like idiots.

D   *Jill went for a walk with Jack.* Who said she did? Just because they both fell down the same hill does not even mean they knew each other, or even that their accidents happened the same day.

E   *Jack fell down.* This is nothing *but* the truth – so it is right.

■ *Exercise 1 Multiple choice comprehension*

The rabbit looked through the hole in the fence, saw our fresh green lawn and abandoned its own garden for ours. It did nothing but eat grass for about two hours. It comes every day now and we don't need to mow the lawn half so often.

Question: Why does the rabbit come into our garden?

Possible answers:

A   We have no lawnmower.

B   It wants to eat our grass.

C   The grass is always greener on the other side.

D   Its owners do not feed it properly.

E   The garden next door has no lawn.

Write down the letter which indicates your choice: *if you write the whole sentence out, your answer must be marked wrong.* (The answer is given on page 232.)

Problem questions

Watch especially for three kinds of question:
1 *those involving a negative word or exception*;
2 *those which involve two or more points at once*;
3 *those which ask about reasons rather than facts.*

1 Negative choices

In these you may easily miss the word "not" or "except".

> There are two kinds of people: those who like egg white and those who don't. I don't. However, eggs are cheap and low on calories, so I make that slithery white rubber a bit more acceptable to my pernickety palate with a thick, disguising sauce of yoghourt, mayonnaise or one of "Safebury's 57 Varieties". And eggs are like Cleopatra: you can't stale their infinite variety – unless, of course, you keep them too long. Scrambled, fried, poached, in omelettes, batter or meringues, "You can't beat an egg" is my slogan.

Question: Which of the following characteristics is not possessed by eggs?
A   They are not expensive.
B   They can be disguised by lots of different sauces.
C   They can be cooked in many different ways.
D   They are fattening.
E   They can cause very different reactions from those who eat them.
Answer: D

If you read that question quickly you might miss the word "not" – and choose the most accurate comment about eggs, rather than the one requested, which is *not* accurate.

2 Choosing more than one

Questions involving more than one point can make you lose your head – especially if the answers dazzle you with numbers.

The new family next door have a lovely dog, a rather well-built labrador called Goldie. The first time she broke through our hedge she came rushing across the flower bed, jumped on me when I was sunbathing and did a pretty good job of washing my face with her tongue. I like dogs so I took it quite well and she *was* still quite small then.

They've had her since she was two months old but, in fact, they "booked" her before she was born. Her mother belonged to their old next-door neighbours and when they heard she was going to have puppies they asked if they could buy one. In the end Goldie was given to them as a sort of goodbye present when they moved.

1 Goldie was some of the following:

(i)	Large	(iv)	Well-trained
(ii)	Affectionate	(v)	Expensive
(iii)	Female		

Which combination is correct?

A	(i), (ii), (iii)	D	(i), (iii), (v)
B	(iii), (iv), (v)	E	(ii), (iv), (v)
C	(ii), (iii), (iv)		

2 Some of the following are true about the writer.

(i) He is fond of dogs.
(ii) He lives alone.
(iii) He was sunbathing when the neighbours moved in.
(iv) He doesn't like gardening.
(v) He has new neighbours.

Which combination is correct?

A	(i), (iv)	D	(ii), (iv)
B	(ii), (v)	E	(i), (v)
C	(ii), (iii)		

Answers: 1A; 2E

a) *First, see how many facts you have to choose.*
In Question 1, about Goldie, each answer contained three parts. So of the five points describing the dog, three were correct and two were *either* wrong *or* unknown.

b) *Then check the facts.*
The dog was clearly referred to as "she", *not* expensive and *not* well-trained.

c) *Now find the numbers which match the facts.*
"Large", "affectionate" and "female" were (i), (ii) and (iii) –
so the answer is A.

d) *It is often quicker to find the wrong points than the right ones.*
If you can find just *one* of them in a possible answer, the whole
answer can be ruled out fast, with no further checking.

3 Finding reasons

It is easier to be sure about what someone does than why he did it – so
be extra careful when a question deals with someone's motives.

Information: I kicked the cat.
Question: What do you know about me, from this fact?

A *I'm the sort of person who kicks cats? No.* I may be 93 and never
have done such a thing before in my life.

B *I'm angry with the cat? No.* I may be angry with my boss or the
tax man – and be taking it out on the cat.

C *I usually like cats because I own one? No.* I may keep pet alligators
and be kicking my neighbour's cat.

D *I'm very clumsy and always falling over the cat? No* evidence to
prove this.

E *I kicked the cat perhaps accidentally, perhaps on purpose? Yes.* This
is the only fact supplied; no deductions are made about my
motives or situation, so E is right.

How to write the answers

Question: When writing your answer to a multiple choice question
do you:

A copy out the whole answer;
B write "Either A or B";
C write "Don't know";
D leave a blank;
E indicate the letter *only* of the answer you have chosen?
Answer: E

Insert the answer you choose by drawing a line between the dots beneath the letter of your choice.

SPECIMEN ANSWER SHEET

Use only an HB pencil
on this sheet

Name of Examination Board:
Examination Level:
English Language

Centre Name   Farnham College

Surname   Castree

First Name(s)   Etheldreda Guinevere

	A	B	C	D	E			A	B	C	D	E
1.	(.)	(.)	(.)	(.)	(.)		16.	(.)	(.)	(.)	(.)	(.)
2.	(.)	(.)	(.)	(.)	(.)		17.	(.)	(.)	(.)	(.)	(.)
3.	(.)	(.)	(.)	(.)	(.)		18.	(.)	(.)	(.)	(.)	(.)
4.	(.)	(.)	(.)	(.)	(.)		19.	(.)	(.)	(.)	(.)	(.)
5.	(.)	(.)	(.)	(.)	(.)		20.	(.)	(.)	(.)	(.)	(.)

DO NOT WRITE ANYTHING IN THIS SPACE

London Board Specimen Answer Sheet

Signature

Do not mark this grid

	Centre Number	Candidate Number

	A	B	C	D	E			A	B	C	D	E
6.	(:)	(:)	(:)	(:)	(:)		21.	(:)	(:)	(:)	(:)	(:)
7.	(:)	(:)	(:)	(:)	(:)		22.	(:)	(:)	(:)	(:)	(:)
8.	(:)	(:)	(:)	(:)	(:)		23.	(:)	(:)	(:)	(:)	(:)
9.	(:)	(:)	(:)	(:)	(:)		24.	(:)	(:)	(:)	(:)	(:)
10.	(:)	(:)	(:)	(:)	(:)		25.	(:)	(:)	(:)	(:)	(:)
11.	(:)	(:)	(:)	(:)	(:)		26.	(:)	(:)	(:)	(:)	(:)
12.	(:)	(:)	(:)	(:)	(:)		27.	(:)	(:)	(:)	(:)	(:)
13.	(:)	(:)	(:)	(:)	(:)		28.	(:)	(:)	(:)	(:)	(:)
14.	(:)	(:)	(:)	(:)	(:)		29.	(:)	(:)	(:)	(:)	(:)
15.	(:)	(:)	(:)	(:)	(:)		30.	(:)	(:)	(:)	(:)	(:)

In *classwork* write down the question number, then the letter of your chosen answer.

In *an examination* you usually have a special answer sheet which lists the possible answers to each question. Mark each letter you choose *using an HB* (= Hard Black) pencil: this is vital as the computer which checks your answers can "read" only HB pencil. Each examination paper gives instructions about how to mark your choices on the answer sheet: sometimes across each letter you choose, sometimes underneath or by the side of it. Look at an old question paper set by your examination board so that you have an idea of what is expected of you. *Always read the instructions on your own examination paper* when you get it, just in case there has been a change.

Remember: if you fill in your answers wrongly, the computer cannot read what you write!

Timing

Concentrate on being accurate and fast.

One board allows 75 minutes for 60 questions on three different passages: one rather easy, one harder and one harder still. This gives you fifteen minutes to read the passages and only one minute to consider each set of five possible answers! You must train hard:

1 Begin with short exercises and plenty of time – about 30 minutes for 10 questions.
2 Then try slightly longer, harder exercises – say 15 questions in 30 minutes – and keep decreasing your time.
3 Finally, tackle *three* different passages, each with about 20 questions, in 75 minutes.

If you have no idea which answer to choose take a gamble.

2 Language: apostrophes

An apostrophe does two *different* jobs: *it shows that a letter is missing* and it *shows ownership.*
It *never* makes a word plural – so do not put an apostrophe in front of every letter -s in sight! It is far better to miss one out when you really need one than to use too many, so: "if in doubt, do without" (and that applies to commas too).

Missing letters

If you leave out a letter on *purpose*, prove it by putting an apostrophe in to mark the spot.

you'll	= you will		ma'am	= madam
I'm	= I am	*	won't	= will not
you've	= you have	*	don't	= do not
two o'clock	= two of the clock	*	daren't	= dare not

(*For more about words ending in "n't", see Unit one, page 31–33.)

Ownership

Use an apostrophe like this:
1 *write the name of the owner* (or owners)
2 *add an apostrophe at the end of it*
3 *ADD -s (for singular)* if there is one *single* owner, but
   DO NOT *add an -s* if there is *more* than one owner.
For example:

ONE (*single*) OWNER	MORE THAN ONE OWNER
the dog's tail	the dogs' tails
my friend's house	my friends' houses
the country's king	the countries' kings
the girl's purse	the girls' purses

Always finish writing out the name of the owner *before* writing the apostrophe, *even* when the owner's name ends in -s, otherwise you change the normal spelling of someone's name:

the teaching of Jesus	= Jesus's teaching
the memory of Miles	= Miles's memory

■ *Exercise 2 Apostrophes*

Re-write the following passages, inserting an apostrophe wherever it is needed to show that a letter is missing.

a) When Im visiting your house its easy to see youre a good cook. Theres always something interesting to eat yet youll always turn out tove spent less that Ive spent on my shopping. Didnt John once say youd cooked a fantastic three-course meal on one gas ring? Thats the kind of cook Id like to be.

b) Theres no point in ringing them up, if theyre coming theyll have left home already and if theyre not coming I dont want to talk to people whod let us down at the last minute. Youre only wasting your time and my money. Anyway, theyre only half an hour late and its not as if theyve never been late before. Joes probably had a puncture – or hes had to work later than usual, thats happened to me often enough.

■ *Exercise 3 Apostrophes*

a) Each of the following owners is singular: write the plural version.
   For example: *one dog's lead* (singular) *two dogs' leads* (plural)

one gardener's spade	one saucepan's handle
one car's horn	one bible's cover
one jury's decision	one wife's worry
one duchess's tiara	one husband's doubt
one cat's fleas	one radio's switch

b) Change each of the following plural words to the singular:
   For example: *the cooks' aprons* (plural) *the cook's apron* (singular)

the houses' gardens	the programmes' producers
the zoos' elephants	the slimmers' exercises
the passports' pictures	the athletes' trainers
the papers' reporters	the secretaries' sandwiches
the councillors' appointments	the window dressers' dummies

Plural exceptions

A few plural words need an apostrophe to show ownership *and* an -s.
For example:

men's shoes   children's socks   people's rights

women's hats   mice's tails

These are words which change a vowel when they move from singular to plural – for example, "man" becomes "men" – but this rarely crops up except for the cases listed here.

When NOT to use an apostrophe

1 *Ownership words.* A few words are used *only* to show ownership and *never* need an apostrophe, even when they end in -s.

mine	ours
his	yours
hers	theirs
	whose

never have an apostrophe

2 *Twin words.* Sometimes two words can sound exactly the same as each other but mean very different things.
Here an apostrophe shows a missing letter – *not* ownership. For example:

Apostrophe	*NO Apostrophe*
it's (= it is)	its (= belonging to it)
they're (= they are)	their (= belonging to them)
you're (= you are)	your (= belonging to you)
who's (= who is)	whose (= belonging to someone just named or not known)

■ *Exercise 4 Apostrophes*

Insert apostrophes where they are needed in the following passage:

That couples two children arent like ours: theyve been so successful at school its amazing. The boy passed his "O" Levels last summer, nine of them, Ive seen his certificate, and the girls clever as well. Id like to think Davids going to pass his exams too, but I dont think theres much hope of that. Jeans got four "O" Levels, shes going to resit the others in June – though whose idea was that? Not hers Im sure, shes just keen to start work.

■ Exercise 5 Apostrophes

Fill the gaps in the following with the correct words:

a) Don't worry, I know _____ (their, they're) going to be there.

b) Can you lend me _____ (your, you're) screwdrivers, please?

c) The council is trying to shut _____ (its, it's) eyes to the problem, but _____ (its, it's) not going to go away as easily as that.

d) I've just seen the man _____ (whose, who's) buying the house next door. _____ (Its, It's) obvious he's not short of money, his car is twice the size of _____ (ours, our's).

e) _____ (Its, It's) _____ (your, you're) turn to wash up, I've been doing it all week and _____ (your, you're) not so busy you can't spare ten minutes.

3 Comprehension: tables and graphs

Lists or diagrams can include a lot of facts without looking complicated. Look at the following:

Version A
From 1982 until 1985 Allied Canneries (UK) employed 263 men and 13 women at their plant in Huddersfield but, because of a decrease in sales, 63 of these were made redundant the following year, when 3 women and 60 men lost their jobs. Meanwhile the firm's factory in Luton, which opened with only 89 workers in 1981, 37 of them female, was expanding rapidly: in the year when 63 jobs were lost at Huddersfield, an extra 69 men and 29 women were employed at Luton.

Version B   Table 1
Employment figures for Allied Canneries (UK) 1982 and 1986

Year	Huddersfield site		Luton site	
	Males	*Females*	*Males*	*Females*
1982	263	13	52	37
1986	203	10	121	66

So when you have a table or graph to work on, *never* think that you should cope with it at a glance just because it does not take up much space. Take plenty of time to study it.
Try to see – *what kinds* of information are given
– *how* that information is arranged
– *trends* in the changes shown
Answer questions – using complete *sentences*
– concentrating on getting the *facts* right

What information is given?

Study headings *first*. For a table these are usually at the top; for a graph look at the axes (the bottom line and the line up the left-hand side) to see what is being measured.

How is the information arranged?

Expect the basic information to be in the top line of a table and in the *left*-hand column (where the years are listed in Table 1). Changes then come further down or across to the right.

So in a bus timetable the basic information, the names of the bus stops, is on the left; the later it is, the further to the right you look for the time of the next bus.

■ *Exercise 6 Comprehension: tables*

Using the United Villages Bus Company timetable (Table 2) opposite answer the following questions *in complete sentences – NOT note form.*

a) How many stops does the bus make on this route after leaving the bus station?
b) At what time does the first bus leave Horsfall Way each morning?
c) To arrive at Moggerhanger Walk by 9.00 am, what time bus should you take from St Mary Street?
d) How many buses stop at Jenner Road each day?
e) At which period during the day is this route
  i) busiest?
  ii) quietest?

Exercise 6 Table 2

UNITED VILLAGES BUS COMPANY – SERVICE 105								
Bus Station	6:00	6:50	7:40	8:30	Then	16:30	Then	19:30
Dane Street	6:03	6:53	7:43	8:33	every	16:33	every	19:33
High Street	6:10	7:00	7:50	8:40	2 hours	16:40	30	19:40
St Mary Street	6:15	7:05	7:55	8:45	until:	16:45	mins	19:45
Gold Street	6:18	7:08	7:58	8:48		16:48	until	19:48
Jenner Road	6:22	7:12	8:02	8:52		16:52		19:52
Horsfall Way	6:28	7:18	8:08	8:58		16:58		19:58
Chaucer Walk	6:34	7:24	8:14	9:04		16:04		20:04
Husband's Bosworth	6:39	7:29	8:19	9:09		16:09		20:09
Moggerhanger Walk	6:45	7:35	8:25	9:15		16:15		20:15

■ *Exercise 7 Tables*

Look at Table 3 opposite.

a) How many subjects does this student study?
b) If students learn best early in the working day, and least at the end of it, which subject has:
   i) the most useful time slots?
   ii) the least useful time slots?
c) On which days does this student work most hours?
d) How many hours a week are provided for:
   i) Maths?
   ii) English?
   iii) History?
e) Which subject is given the fewest hours on the timetable?
f) i) On which day does this timetable seem to be most badly planned?
   ii) What has been forgotten by the planners?

What trends are shown in the changes?

Exercise 6(e) asked you to decide when bus route 105 was busiest and when quietest; Exercise 7(f) asked you to find fault with the planning of the student timetable. Questions like these usually carry high marks and are usually asked at the end, after some purely factual questions which should help you to get to know the situation.

Exercise 7   *Table 3*

STUDENT TIMETABLE

DAY	9-10	10-11	11-12	12-1	1-2	2-3	3-4	4-5
Monday					MATHS	MATHS	FRENCH	PHYSICS
Tuesday	ENGLISH	ENGLISH	FRENCH		HISTORY	HISTORY	MATHS	PHYSICS
Wednesday	GEOGRAPHY	ENGLISH	BIOLOGY	BIOLOGY		PRIVATE STUDY	PHYSICS	PHYSICS
Thursday	GEOGRAPHY	GEOGRAPHY	PRIVATE STUDY		ENGLISH	ENGLISH	MATHS	RELIGIOUS STUDIES
Friday	MATHS	MATHS	HISTORY	BIOLOGY	BIOLOGY	FRENCH	PHYSICS	ENGLISH
Saturday	GEOGRAPHY	HISTORY	FRENCH	RELIGIOUS STUDIES				

A graph is often even simpler to understand than a table, because you can see the changes it describes, without searching for them. Here too, the basic situation is indicated on the left, with changes further to the right – but of course instead of looking down columns, as in a table, you expect to start with the bottom line and follow the lines *up* from there.

The following graph gives an idea of how it feels to be living in London for twelve months.

Diagram 1

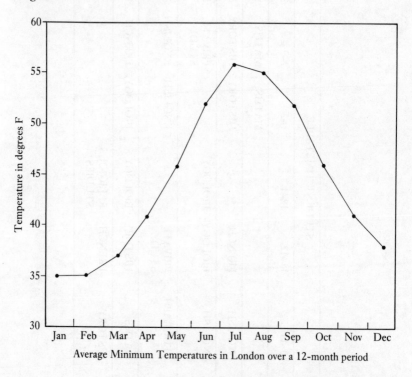

Average Minimum Temperatures in London over a 12-month period

Obviously high points, in July and August, indicate one-sweater weather, while the January temperature, predictably, suggests a three-sweater situation. However, this is a deduction. Lists and diagrams give you just facts and figures which you have to interpret for yourself.

They can also give you too little information to form a balanced view. London's minimum temperature seemed to change a lot according to Diagram 1, but if compared with the winter nosedive in Peking, London temperature changes might look rather undramatic.

Diagram 2

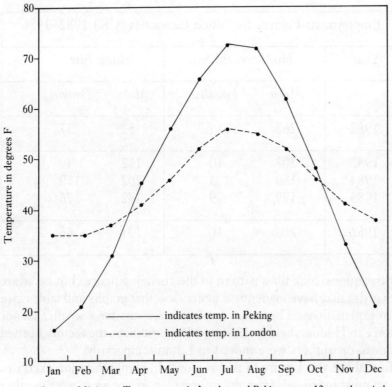

Average Minimum Temperatures in London and Peking over a 12-month period

■ *Exercise 8 Tables*

Explain whether employment figures seem to be getting higher or
lower at Huddersfield and at Luton
a) using Table 1 on page 163;
b) using Table 4 below.

Table 4

Employment Figures for Allied Canneries (UK) 1982–1986				
Year	Huddersfield Site		Luton Site	
	Males	*Females*	*Males*	*Females*
1982	263	13	52	37
1983	203	10	112	49
1984	159	3	202	119
1985	179	9	142	76
1986	203	10	121	66

Be cautious: look for a pattern in the changing figures but be aware
that you may have inadequate figures *and* that graphs and tables give
no explanations. There may be simple reasons for a smaller labour
force in Huddersfield in 1984 and 1985: perhaps the factory burned
down, or workers were moved to Luton temporarily.

In real life you can try to find reasons. In comprehension exercises
you must judge *only* from the information given: *never* refer to other
facts which you happen to know unless a question *clearly* invites
you to do so. Your answers to questions of judgment, therefore,
should include phrases like:

    it seems as though . . .

    from the figures provided, it appears that . . .

    it is possible that . . .

■ *Exercise 9*

The following graph shows sales of two new pet foods in the Greater London Area: Bonzai Chunky Meat and Bonzai Crunchies.

Diagram 3

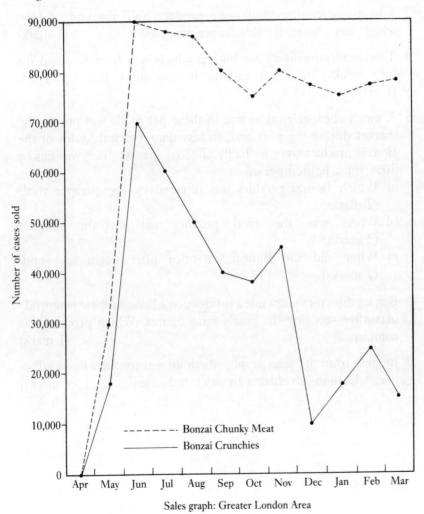

Sales graph: Greater London Area

1 Both products were launched, in April, with a two-month advertising campaign on television: what was its effect on sales of Bonzai Crunchies?   (1 mark)

2 During the campaign a competition offered customers some very attractive prizes: entry coupons were printed on labels of one of the two products. Which do you think it was? (1 mark)

3 Advertising continued for one product until the end of July: which was chosen for this longer promotion?   (1 mark)

4 Television advertising for both products was later resumed for four weeks: in which month do you think this happened? (1 mark)

5 A much cheaper rival to one of these pet foods was put on the market during the year and, in less than a month, sales of the Bonzai product were so badly affected that its price was cut by 30% for a limited period.
  a) Which Bonzai product was affected by the cheaper rival? (2 marks)
  b) When was the rival product put on the market? (2 marks)
  c) When did the Bonzai cut-price offer begin and end? (2 marks)

6 Bonzai directors suspended production of one of their two products after studying the year's sales figures. Which product was continued?   (1 mark)

7 Judging from the sales graph, which do you consider more effective, television advertising or price reduction?   (4 marks)

4 Words: common mistakes

That kind of thing ... Those kinds of things

If you talk about a group of things, all the words about that group should be singular, because you are thinking of them as *one* group.

RIGHT: I don't like *that kind* of *book*.

WRONG: I don't like *those kind* of *books*.

If you are thinking of two groups, or more than two, *all* the words involved now become plural.

RIGHT: I don't enjoy *those kinds* of *films*.

Always avoid a mixture of singular and plural.

WRONG: *Those kind* of *mistakes* drive me mad.

RIGHT: *This kind* of *mistake* ...

OR *Those kinds* of *mistakes* ...

That, so

"That" means *which* (not how many or how much) – so don't use "that" when you need "so" or "very".

RIGHT: I like **that** ring, not the other one.

She asked for some of **that** vintage cider and I'm sure she's only twelve.

WRONG: She's **that** stupid she'd believe the Martians had landed if I said so on April 1st.

The last example was wrong because it tried to use "that" to say *how much* stupidity there was: "so" should have been used.

Alot

The word "alot" does not exist, neither does "abit" or "alittle"

WRONG: I don't want *alot* of money.

RIGHT: I don't want *a lot* of money.

Worse, worst: better, best

When things increase in awfulness they go from **bad** to **worse** (*never* say "more bad") to **worst** (*never* say "more worse").
For example:

John's a bad boy – he's been expelled;

Jacob's a worse boy, he's been expelled twice;

Joss is the worst of the lot, no one's got him into a school yet!

If there are only two people to think about, use **bad** and **worse** (and leave out worst). For example:

Joe is bad at maths but Kate is worse.

When things increase in niceness they go from **good** to **better** (*never* say "more good") to **best** (*never* say "more better").
For example:

Anna is a good girl – she runs errands for me:

Amrit is a better girl – she does a lot of housework;

Aisha is the best of the lot – she rewired the house before breakfast!

Again, if there are only two to compare with each other, use **good** and **better** (and leave out best)

Mixing up tenses

Tense means *time*: you show *when* things happen by choosing different forms of all the "action words", as well as by using time words like "now", "yesterday", and "last August".
For example:

I **can see** him coming **now**. (*Present tense*)

I **saw** him coming **yesterday**. (*Past tense*)

I **shall see** him when he comes **tomorrow**. (*Future tense*)

Never change tenses by accident: it can be very confusing.
For example:

I **see** him coming **now**: he **looks** so ill, his skin **is** yellow and he was so thin!

The words in bold type are in the present tense, but then the writer switched to the past tense, using "was" instead of "is", so you cannot tell whether the man was thin *once*, but not any more – or whether he is still thin.

Adding -ly

slow or slowly?   cruel or cruelly?
quick or quickly?   hungry or hungrily?

Which of these should you use – and when?

i) *To describe people, things and places* you need one kind of word – an **adjective**.

For example: slow   cruel
                    quick   hungry

ii) *to describe actions* you need a different kind of word – an **adverb**.
  For example:

slow<u>ly</u>   cruel<u>ly</u>
quick<u>ly</u>   hungri<u>ly</u>

These often end in -<u>ly</u>.

In the following four examples the words in bold type are action words – or **verbs**. It is the *action* which is described not the person so adverbs are needed here.

WRONG   RIGHT
She **got** there quick.   She **got** there quick**ly**.
He **did** that very nice.   He **did** that very nice**ly**.
He **said** it so polite.   He **said** it so polite**ly**.
Didn't they do good?   **Didn't** they **do well**?

■ *Exercise 10 Common mistakes*

Correct the mistakes in the following sentences.

a) Do you really want that kind of cable television programmes?
b) These kind of people make me ashamed of being white.
c) Don't tell me it was those sort you wanted all the time!
d) You don't really eat these sort of snails do you?
e) You don't want alot do you? The best car in the showroom for the price of a broken down Mini and you complain! Alot of people say that my prices will get me in the bankruptcy court before long, and the overheads are that high. You won't get alot of dealers letting you have a car like this that cheap.

■ *Exercise 11 Common mistakes*

Insert "that" or "so" in each of the spaces in the following passage:

It was _____ cold outside I wore _____ new coat you gave me, the one which was _____ expensive, but the hall was _____ hot, there were _____ many people there, _____ Jean and I left our coats in the cloakroom.

Later, when the girl asked for my ticket, I couldn't find it: she was _____ cross, she said the cloakroom was far too big for her to search for one coat, especially when there were _____ many there _____ night.

I was determined to find _____ ticket but there were _____ many pieces of paper on the floor and Jean had to rush off to catch her bus. _____ boy from King Street saw me looking worried and helped me find it, but there was _____ much rubbish it took ages and I missed the last bus. _____ John walked home with me, although it's _____ far from his house. But it's over ten miles and I couldn't walk _____ fast as I usually do as my shoes hurt. I'm sorry you were worried, but two a.m. isn't _____ late.

■ *Exercise 12 Common mistakes*

Correct the mistakes in the following sentences:

a) Jay is that depressed: last week he lost his job and now his parents had thrown him out. It couldn't be a more bad situation — he's taking his A Levels next month.
b) My first driving lesson was the worse forty minutes I've ever lived through!
c) Jay is the better looking one, if you think of all the boys at the club. He's better than anyone else at rugby too!
d) I know I didn't like your blue dress but that one's worst!
e) That kid next door has gone from bad to worst: he actually swore at old Mrs Bailey in the corner shop this morning.
f) I've had two jobs, the first was in banking and that was the safest I admit, but being a lion tamer in a safari park is the best thing I've tried for excitement. One lion looks much like any other after a while, but they aren't the worse conversationalists I've met and they move faster than my old bank manager did.

■ *Exercise 13 Tenses*

What tense is used in each of the following sentences: past, present or future?

a) I'm going out now, before the shops shut.
b) He didn't tell me he was married already.
c) It's easy to see which is which; Jake is a good six inches taller than Phil.
d) I shall be in Manchester for Christmas, so I shan't be able to come with you to that party after all.
e) You were in college last week, I saw you.
f) The Prime Minister is here to open the new block.
g) Did you really remember the passports?

■ *Exercise 14 Tenses*

Make any changes you need to keep the following sentences in the *present* tense.

a) I liked Lena but I hadn't like her mother much.
b) The puppies are all black, except Biff and he was black and brown.
c) Cars were essential to our modern way of life, otherwise we shall take far too long in getting to places, we can't spend enough time working if we have taken two hours to walk to our jobs and another two hours to walk home.
d) Gardening is a marvellous hobby: it helps you to keep healthy and it provided you with flowers and vegetables as an extra bonus.

■ *Exercise 15 Adjectives and adverbs*

a) What do you use to describe each of these words, an **adjective** (for people and things) or an **adverb** (for actions)?

Superman	climbed	bully	lizard
chocolate	coughed	punched	rub
fetched	elephant	towel	slept
casserole	junk shop	laughing	concentrate
mistake	interrupted	sneezed	Jane

b) Supply three describing words for each word listed in (a). Make sure they are all the right kind to suit the words they are describing.

5 Spelling: words often confused

1 W-**ea**-ther means *wind and rain* (and looks like f-**ea**-ther).
W-**he**-ther means *if* (it looks rather like t-e-ther).
Try saying "whether the weather" over and over again to your-self, making sure you *say* the -h in the right place.

2 Qui-**et** means *peaceful* (and rhymes with di-**et**).
Qu-**ite** means *rather* (and rhymes with sp-**ite**).
Practise saying "qu-**ite** spiteful, this qui-**et** di-**et**".

3 **New** means *the opposite of old* (and rhymes with few).
Knew means *was aware of* (and unfortunately sounds *just* like its twin!)
Try saying **King Kanute**
              k-new
              a canny thing or two
to remind you that **k**-now and **k**-new have a **k**, or make up a short rhyme of your own to help you remember it.

4 Pas-**t** is about *time* (remember to match the -t).
Pas-**sed** is what *someone did* (match the -d).

At ten **past** two Tom's troubles were in the **past**.
Dracula **passed** the dungeon door with dread.

5 Princi-**pal** means *chief* (could be a **pal**).
Princi-**ple** means *rule* (not always **ple**asant).

The princi**pal** reason for the palace party was to meet the princi**pals** of polytechnics.
The disci**ple** pleaded that living for **ple**asure was against his princi**ples**.

■ Exercise 16 Spelling

Choose **weather, whether, quite, quiet, new** or **knew** to fill each of the following blanks:

a) In this kind of dull _____ I never know _____ to take an umbrella.

b) It's so _____ at home now Ben's away at college: the house is _____ immaculate but it's also _____ boring.

c) You'll never make me doubt that the dog _____ what I was saying, I'm _____ sure of it.

d) Is that today's _____spaper or _____ an old one?

e) Everyone suddenly went _____ and he _____ he shouldn't have said it.

f) _____ you like it or not, the neighbours are _____ happy that we've changed our noisy old car for _____ a _____ one.

■ Exercise 17 Spelling

Choose the right word to fill the blanks in the following sentences:

a) That man has no moral _____ (principals/principles) if he believes that the _____ (principal/principle) aim in life is to make money.

b) I realised I hadn't _____ (past/passed) my driving test when I _____ (past/passed) a halt sign without stopping. From _____ (past/passed) experience I knew too that I should not have _____ (past/passed) that lorry on a blind bend.

c) The _____ (principal/principle) of the college has not in the _____ (past/passed) interviewed students who have _____ (past/passed) their final examinations.

6 Exercises for revision

■ Exercise 18 Multiple choice comprehension

Read the following passage, then select the correct answers to the questions.

He stared at the advertisement hard. He couldn't believe what he had seen.

Slowly, he checked the other notices near it: "For Sale, Gas Cooker, 4 burners, eye-level grill – nearly new"; ". . . Mother's Friend twin pushchair, four years old . . . immaculate . . .". Those were real enough, he thought, the cast-offs of the middle aged and middle class, drifting downwards in desirability as old age or improved technology made them less attractive. Then, incredibly, there was that ordinary postcard, offering just what he thought he'd never find. "Three-roomed first floor flat, + garage, near town centre, owner emigrating. Central heating, fitted kitchen, bath + shower. Long lease. £20,000."

His mouth went dry with anxiety. It must have gone. He couldn't be that lucky. After six months of living in digs that smelled of damp cabbage and doing the rounds of the estate agents every weekend, there'd been nothing. Now, wedged between a tired gas cooker and a pushchair smelling of soggy rusks – and worse – there was the flat he'd longed for, at a price his building society thought he could afford. His hand shaking, he scribbled the phone number on that morning's "Lucky Gift if **you** Reply **now**!" envelope and fumbled for change.

One phone box, three tenpences and a short, breathless drive later, he was looking at The Perfect Flat. On the first floor of a Victorian mansion, its three rooms were beautiful: elegant high ceilings, fitted carpets included for a modest sum, the windows sheltered from noise and nosy neighbours by double glazing and some beautiful elm trees.

"It's just about what I wanted." His voice sounded far away, unreal, ridiculously calm when he was so desperate to pay the deposit, sign the contract, keep out higher bidders with guard dogs. No more damp cabbage, no more hostile looks because he'd come in after eleven the night before. No more reminders that radios should *not* be used between eleven pm and eight in the morning. No more grotty furniture and black mould in the corner by the wardrobe.

"It's a lovely flat," she said. "We're going to Kingston and have to sell – though I *shall* miss it. There is one thing, only a small thing, but one or two people seem to have been a bit put off by it. It's ... I ought to tell you. Well, it's ..." She looked at me awkwardly. "It sounds odd, but you see – there's a ghost!"

1 Why did the man re-read several notices?
   A He had not read them properly before.
   B He had not found what he was looking for.
   C He was interested in buying a pushchair.
   D He couldn't believe what he had seen.
   E He found them interesting.

2 The man is each of the following except:
   A anxious   D a bad driver
   B living in lodgings   E looking for privacy
   C ready to have a mortgage

3 Which of the following phrases does not describe the flat accurately?
   A on the first floor   D near the town centre
   B has a gas cooker   E has high ceilings
   C on a long lease

4 The woman selling the flat was all of the following except:
   A anxious to leave it   D fond of the flat
   B moving to Kingston   E on the telephone
   C honest

5 Which of the following words is closest in meaning to "immaculate" in line 5?
   A undamaged   D spotless
   B waterproof   E highly desirable
   C easily cleaned

6 The final situation in this passage could not be accurately described as:
   A shocking   D worrying
   B unusual   E predictable
   C weird

■ *Exercise 19 Apostrophes*

In the following passage apostrophes are *sometimes used* where they should not be and *missed out* when they are needed. Correct all the mistakes you can find *and* explain why they were wrong.

> You're not going without me, Im not going to be long. Its far too early yet and Ill be ready soon. Ive only got to finish washing up, cook the plum's and then wash your shirt's. Why dont you watch television while youre waiting? Oh! Of course you cant, the control knobs arent working, but theres you'r portable set, thats all right. Those people you like are on now, the funny one's – you know, the one's who always end up throwing custard pies in each other's faces. Johns keen on them too. I'll be ready to go out when thats over.

■ *Exercise 20 Apostrophes*

Write a separate sentence for each of the following words, showing the difference in meanings of words which sound the same.

whose	their	government's	journalists'	tomatoes
who's	they're	governments'	journalist's	tomato's

■ *Exercise 21 Comprehension: tables*

Answer the following questions in complete sentences, basing your answers on Table 5.

a) Which of the following building programmes seems most urgent, in town B, during the next four years?
   i) Lower schools   iii) Upper schools
   ii) Middle schools   iv) Day centres for pensioners

b) In one town the proportion of people of 65 and over is soon likely to be greater than that of people 16 and under. Which town is this?

c) Which town seems to have a roughly equal number of people in each age range listed?

d) Which town needs more middle school places most urgently?

Exercise 21   Table 5   Showing age distribution amongst young and old sections of the population in four towns

Name of town	Total population	No. of population				No. of school places available				No. of day centre places for pensioners
		under 5	60 to 64	65 to 75	over 75	Lower School (5–8 yr olds)	Middle School (9–12 yr olds)	Upper School (13+ yr olds)	Total School Pop.	
A	24,000	6,000	3,000	1,000	1,000	1,000	2,000	1,000	4,000	1,000
B	68,000	17,000	6,000	3,000	2,000	7,000	5,000	3,000	15,000	3,000
C	99,000	7,000	19,000	9,000	8,000	7,000	8,000	8,000	23,000	2,000
D	200,000	21,000	20,000	21,000	18,000	21,000	24,000	21,000	66,000	30,000

e) Judging from the school numbers, which town spends the largest proportion of its education expenditure on middle schools?

f) One town has a particularly inadequate day centre provision for citizens of 65 and over. Which is it?

g) In one town, far sighted parents want councillors to increase upper school places. Which town is this most likely to be?

h) Six years ago each town council forecast a large percentage increase in the need for playschool places for children under five. Which councils seem to have been wrong?

i) Each town has, for many years, arranged special courses to prepare people for imminent retirement. Which town has least need to increase the number of courses it runs?

■ Exercise 22 Common mistakes

Re-write the following sentences, correcting wherever it is necessary and underlining your corrections.

a) Maria is the kind of girl alot of parents would be proud of; she's the sort of girl employers like, boys notice and other girls weren't so keen on. She was the youngest of four children, much younger than the other three and the one nobody ever blames for anything – she always sounded so convincing when she blames one of the others that nobody ever doubts her.

b) Jake has had alot of trouble since he left school. He was best off before he left, though it's that hard for him to admit it. Did you mind talking to him? He couldn't be worst off than he is now and he'd listen to your advice. He's that depressed about having nothing to do and never having alot of money: I know people must always be asking you to do these sort of things and he did leave sudden, but I'm sure he really loved to come back if you gave him the chance.

c) The woman went slow and cautious over to the limp body: it lay motionless – then a shudder runs through it, quick, like an electric charge; the groaning begins again. It would be over by now if she'd sent for the doctor at the beginning, he'd be here and the agony would be over. Now she waits, fearing the worse, sharing the pain, till help came.

■ Exercise 23 Spelling

Fill each blank with one of the words supplied after it in brackets.

a) I haven't _____ (past/passed) but I shall try again in November. In the _____ (past/passed) I wouldn't have bothered, but now I have _____ (past/passed) the stage of hurt pride, and I know that I nearly _____ (past/passed).

b) The old woman _____ (new/knew) that if she seemed _____ (quiet/quite) cheerful they would stop fussing and let her have some peace and _____ (quiet/quite).

c) All's reasonably _____ (quiet/quite) on the western front, but all hell's breaking out over the _____ (new/knew) border posts in the east. I _____ (new/knew) it would, _____ (weather/whether) they denied it or not.

d) In this kind of _____ (weather/whether) the best thing to do is plan a few _____ (quiet/quite) evenings with a book or two and leave the gardening till it's _____ (quiet/quite) warm again.

e) The _____ (new/knew) girl asked _____ (weather/whether) she had to buy her own textbooks. She was _____ (quiet/quite) relieved to hear that she could borrow them free.

f) The _____ (principal/principle) ingredient is peat, with a little bone meal added, on the _____ (principal/principle) that extra nutrition is worth having.

UNIT SEVEN

1 Factual writing

Instructions

Instructions must be easy to understand. After reading them, *any* reader must *know* what to do even when doing the task for the first time. You can help by:

1 using simple words and short sentences
2 inventing a title which says exactly what the instructions are for
3 providing clear diagrams where helpful
4 keeping each step in the process separate
5 putting the steps in a sensible order
6 mentioning anything which keeps the reader on the right lines
7 leaving spaces – it is hard to follow words packed together.

When you are writing instructions, you need to plan logically:

1 *Make a list of everything to be done.* The reader will not know what to do unless *you* have told him.

2 *Write your first draft.* Leave gaps so you can make changes later.

3 *Read the first draft through.* Can you help the reader even more? By using simpler words? By breaking the job down into smaller steps?

4 *Write the final version.* It will probably be very different from your first effort.

■ Exercise 1 Instructions

Write instructions on how to do THREE of the following:

a) wash your hair
b) make an omelette
c) change a car wheel
d) make a local telephone call from a public box
e) iron a shirt or a blouse

■ *Exercise 2 Comparing sets of instructions*

These two sets of instructions tell how to wire a plug. Which is better, and *why?*

a) *Fixing a plug*

Buy the kind of plug you need and take off the top. Fit the flex in far enough at one end so the three wires reach the holes they have to be fitted in. Screw each wire in the proper hole. You can tell which one is which because they are labelled. Each wire is also a different colour. When each wire is screwed down and there are no bits sticking out to touch each other, screw the top back on and switch on.

b) *How to fix a 13-amp 3-pin plug to a length of 3-core flex*

i) Strip about 50 mm of the outer covering from the flex, revealing the three coloured wires inside.

ii) Remove the top of the plug by loosening the central screw.

iii) Take out the cartridge fuse.

iv) At the first entry point is a small clamp strip held by two screws. Remove one, loosen the other.

v) Insert enough flex for each coloured wire to reach its correct terminal with about 12 mm to spare. Trim off the surplus wire.

The terminal top centre, marked E, is connected to the green and yellow **earth** wire.

The terminal top right, marked L, is connected to the brown **live** wire.

The terminal bottom left, marked N, is connected to the blue **neutral** wire.

It is very important that these connections are made correctly.

vi) Screw down the clamp strip to hold the flex into position.

vii) Trim about 6 mm of the coloured insulation from the end of each wire. Do not cut through the copper strands inside.

viii) Twist the copper strands in each wire to make the tips more compact. Put each twisted end into the hole at the *correct* terminal. Tighten the screw at each terminal to secure wire.

ix) No loose strands of copper wire should now be visible, only the coloured wires leading to the three terminals.

x) Insert a cartridge fuse of the rating needed by the appliance.

xi) Replace the top of the plug and tighten the fixing screw.

■ *Exercise 3   Instructions*

Write instructions on THREE of the following:

a) Starting a car or motorcycle and moving off on to a main road.
b) Hanging wallpaper.
c) Making pastry.
d) Mending a puncture in a bicycle tyre.
e) Laying a lawn.

Factual descriptions

A factual description usually has longer paragraphs than a set of instructions. The paragraphs are not normally numbered but a logical order is still important.

1 Name what you are describing.

2 Explain its purpose or function.

3 Describe what it looks like.

4 Say how it is used.

5 Add any special features.

Descriptions should be business-like and brief. Here is an example. It is not fun to read but it presents the facts in a clear, concise way.

The XJ16 desk-mounted photocopier weighs about 12 kilograms. It is 60 cm wide, 50 cm deep and 30 cm high increasing to a maximum of 70 cm when the flap on the top of the machine is raised to position papers to be copied. Material for copying is placed on top of the machine, above a clear glass plate, and the hinged plastic flap is then lowered to cover the material and hold it in place. Arrows at the edge of the glass plate are labelled to show the exact positions where papers of different sizes should be placed so that the whole document is copied. Up to 10 copies can be printed during one operation.

There are three control knobs in the top right-hand corner of the machine. The white knob is labelled "off/on" and must be turned to the right before each operation.

The red knob is marked around its circumference with the numbers 1 to 10. The number of copies is selected by turning this red knob clockwise, until the required number is at the top, just beneath the red arrow on the front of the machine.

The blue knob, labelled "Start printing", is then pushed in. The machine will produce the number of copies indicated by the red knob which will turn during the process, returning to the number 1.

To stop the machine during printing, the white knob should be turned to the "off" position.

The machine costs £2,500 which includes a one-year guarantee of labour and parts and 10,000 sheets of copying paper.

Before writing a factual description, think who is going to read it. What will the reader *need* to know about the person, thing or process you are about to describe?

■ *Exercise 4 Main points in a factual description*

List the main points that should be covered in describing EACH of the following:

a) A local factory *or* supermarket
b) The town *or* village where you live
c) A house *or* flat
d) A book, film *or* television programme

■ *Exercise 5 Factual description*

Write a factual description of EACH of the following:

a) Yourself – for a pen-friend
b) Yourself – for a possible employer
c) The college where you are a student – for the college prospectus
d) Your job – for somebody interested in the same type of work

Look at this description of a person.

> The man is in his late twenties, about 6 feet tall and slim. He has fair hair, grey eyes and a scar on his left cheek. He speaks with a Cornish accent. He was last seen near Grant Hospital in Sedgeley, wearing blue jeans and a green anorak. The man is dangerous and likely to be armed. He should not be approached by a member of the public.

Where would you find such a description? Clearly the answer is – on a police Wanted poster. Some of the information might be useful for the files of a marriage bureau but the man would be unlikely to find a wife.

Factual descriptions must fit their purpose – in content, language and order.

Advertisements

A job description for an advertisement has to give information about hours, duties and pay. It needs to be brief and eye-catching using large bold type for the features it wants to stress:

LAMBERT & LAMBERT
Architects and Surveyors require a full-time
TYPIST/RECEPTIONIST
from 1st April
£4,000 p.a., pension scheme, 5 day week
Apply in writing to
Mrs J Dean, 36 Needle Court, Cranfield, Beds MS22 3BN

■ *Exercise 6 Advertisements for different purposes*

Write TWO advertisements for the same second-hand car. Both descriptions must be factual but the first should stress quality while the second, quoting a lower price, should emphasise what a bargain the car is and aim for a quick sale.

■ *Exercise 7 Newspaper advertisements*

Write newspaper advertisements for TWO of the following:

a) A companion of the opposite sex
b) A semi-detached house, to go in "Properties for Sale"
c) A home for 23 baby rabbits, to be placed in the Pets section
d) A student looking for weekend work, to go in Jobs Wanted

2 Language: confused writing

It is important to use language clearly. Sometimes you may have a reason for confusing or mystifying a reader but generally you want your meaning to be clear.

Pronouns

Pronouns, the words which replace nouns, can cause confusion. Words like:

he	him	his
she	her	hers
it		its
they	them	their

are useful because they help you avoid boring repetition. Sometimes though, it is hard to know which noun is referred to. Look at this sentence:

He put on his coat because it was cold.

"It" could mean "his coat" but more likely the writer means "the weather" although this is not mentioned. There is no real confusion. But look at the next example:

He sat on the radiator because it was cold.

The sense is not clear. "It" could refer to "the radiator" or the weather.

■ Exercise 8 Confusing sentences

Why are the following sentences confusing?

a) Monica told her great aunt that she looked awful in a bikini.
b) The Browns met the Robinsons and they hated them.
c) Julia asked her sister if she had finished with her book.
d) Those workers make cars but they are very slow.
e) He dropped the egg on the china tortoise and cracked its shell.
f) Mrs Lazarus wiped the windscreen because it was misty.
g) Her car collided with an oak tree and it burst into flames.
h) Beryl met Mrs Shuffle and she said to her that she was getting fat and she would have to do something about it.

That, which, who, etc.

There are other words which can cause confusion in a reader's mind if used carelessly. These are:

that
which
who   whom
where
when

Here are two sentences:

1 I introduced them to a charming woman with a hairy, cross-eyed husband who was wearing a pink dress.
2 He complained about a little jacket he had bought for his poodle which shrank in the wash.

In these examples the order of words confuses the sense. If "which" and "who" get separated from the words they refer to, there is a chance of confusion. It is easy to re-write the sentences to make the sense clear:

1 I introduced them to a charming woman in a pink dress. She had a hairy, cross-eyed husband.
2 He had bought his poodle a little jacket which he complained shrank in the wash.

Remember: when you use words like which, who and that – make sure they refer to the words you want them to refer to.

"When" and "where" can also cause problems. Here are two questions:

1 Where were you wounded?
2 When did she tell you she would see you?

In the first sentence, "where" could refer to a part of the body or a place. In the second sentence, the "when" could mean the "seeing" or the "telling". Re-writing gets rid of the confusion:
Either In what country were you wounded?
Or   In what part of the body were you wounded?
Either She told you she would see you. When did she tell you?
Or   She told you she would see you. When will she see you?

■ *Exercise 9 Confusing sentences*

Re-write these sentences to make the sense perfectly clear:

a) Where was the baby vaccinated?
b) When did the Admiral suggest that the fleet should sail?
c) We stayed in a hotel with only one lift which contained a thousand people when full.
d) The naturalist had a monkey on her shoulder which was brown and hairy.
e) They hired a band with blue jackets that played "Greensleeves".
f) They live in a house on a hill that was built by their uncle.
g) The small boy with the big ears and the huge mother who is always fighting in the street was kept in after school.
h) He asked for an egg in his pyjamas which had been boiled for three minutes.

Word order

Word order is important in English. Here is an example of how meaning suffers if words are put in the wrong order:

> You can now obtain licences to send cattle to the continent by post.

"by post" is in the wrong place. The sentence should be:

> You can now obtain licences by post to send cattle to the continent.

■ *Exercise 10 Word order causing confusion*

Re-write the following sentences to get the intended sense:

a) He wrote a poem about his girlfriend split into two halves.
b) Mr O'Driscoll saw the boy jumping through a knot-hole in the fence.
c) The writer served chops to his customers swimming in tomato sauce.
d) The judge condemned the prisoner to life imprisonment in a grey wig.
e) You will not catch cold germs walking in the fresh air.
f) The porter delivered a statue of the Queen wearing dungarees.
g) She wrote to her father about the swimming gala in black ink.
h) Old Joe cannot hear a thing you say without a hearing aid.

Brackets and dashes are two types of punctuation which can help your writing.

Brackets

Brackets always come in pairs and they enclose words which seem to be added to a sentence as an afterthought:

The fruits on display (apples, pears and plums) were sold for charity.

The sentence must still make sense if the words between the brackets are removed:

The fruits on display were sold for charity.

Some people enjoy using brackets but too many of them can annoy a reader. It looks as if the writer has not thought carefully before writing.

■ *Exercise 11 Brackets*

Put brackets where they are needed in the following sentences:

a) The aircraft a Spitfire and a Hurricane were relics of the war.
b) There is more about this subject later in the book see page 203.
c) The baby was called Goliath Obadiah what a name! by her parents.
d) The people live in yerts mud huts and hunt yaks for food.
e) Debra painted the bathroom magnolia creamy-white and the hall pink.

Dashes

Dashes can do the same job as brackets but if the words enclosed come at the end of a sentence, the second dash is not need. You would write:

Johnson missed – it seemed easier to score – a gaping open goal.

with two dashes but:

There is one thing I want on holiday – good weather.

with one dash because the sentence ends after "good weather".

■ Exercise 12 Dashes

Put dashes where needed in these sentences:

a) Mary is a really kind woman everybody says so and she will help.
b) I will send him a recipe for slimmer's sponge cake no fat needed.
c) The golden eagle a spectacular sight is found only in Scotland.
d) We received three hundred Christmas cards what a waste of money.
e) My husband don't tell him I told you wears a red nightcap in bed.

Dashes and brackets allow you to slip in a comment which could inform or amuse a reader. If you do it too often, the reader feels interrupted and could lose interest.

3 Factual writing: memoranda, reports and essays

Memoranda

Memoranda is the plural of the word "memorandum". A memorandum or "memo" is a short note sent between people in a firm. The following tips should help you to write good memoranda.

* *Say who the memorandum is from.* You might want an answer.
* *Say who the memorandum is to.* It could be to one or more people.
* *Date the memorandum.* This is important for reference.
* *Give the memorandum a title.* It helps to focus the reader's mind.
* *Write about one subject only.* A memorandum is *not* a letter. If you have two things to write about, send two memoranda.
* Write in direct, business-like English.

Here is an example of a typical memorandum with a normal layout.

> To: All Heads of Department
> From: Canteen Manager   14th September 1986
> **CANTEEN PRICES INCREASE**
> Would you please tell staff in your department that canteen prices will go up by 10% in October? The new prices will apply from the first Monday of the month. I regret this increase but prices have been steady for 13 months although in that time all our costs have risen.

■ Exercise 13 Memoranda

Write memoranda on TWO of the following topics:

a) Inadequacy of staff car parking facilities
b) Organising a retirement party
c) Booking a room
d) Sale of unwanted typewriter
e) New product for sale
f) A works outing to the seaside

Reports

A report is a piece of writing produced after investigation or thought. It is written for a particular person or group. A report is based on fact and description but it may contain opinion and recommendation. You may have a great deal of information available but be selective. Choose:

* What is important for your audience to know.
* What will support any opinions or recommendations you include.

In an examination you will be limited by time so selection is important. A report must be easy to follow. Help the reader by:

* *Giving the report a suitable title.*
* *Arranging the report in a logical order.* Divide it into *short paragraphs.*
* *Writing in simple, direct language.*

■ Exercise 14 Reports

You have been asked to write ONE of the following reports. Make a list of the main points you would include:

a) A report to the council on street lighting in your road.
b) A report to the BCC or ITV on a particular television programme.
c) A report to the maker of a new convenience food.
d) A report to the Safety Council on an electric drill.

Here is a typical examination question on writing reports:

> You are a member of the catering committee at your firm or college. The chairman asks you to write a report on the canteen. Write the report, suggesting improvements to the service.

You might decide to divide this report into 5 sections:
1 Is the canteen a pleasant place to eat in?
2 What sorts of menus are provided?
3 Is the service satisfactory?
4 Is the canteen food of good quality and well-prepared?
5 Are prices reasonable?
Before you write, you need to know what your suggestions will be so that you can support them with evidence. In this case, you might recommend:

a) that the canteen be re-decorated.
b) that a greater variety of dishes be offered.
c) that prices go up to cover the cost of (a) and (b).
The final report might read like this:

HOW TO IMPROVE OUR CANTEEN

This report was written at the request of the Catering Committee chairman. The writer did a survey of the canteen and questioned users and non-users of the canteen while gathering evidence.

1 *Is the canteen a pleasant place to eat?*
The canteen is clean and light. Everybody questioned agreed that it *could* be a good place to eat. Most people thought, however, that re-decoration was needed. The paintwork was described as "drab" and a new lively colour scheme was seen as likely to attract more custom.

2 *What sort of menus are provided?*
There is a different menu for each day of the week but there is no choice. If a person dislikes what is on offer, he must go elsewhere. There is no provision for snacks. Customers must have a full meal. This was seen as a problem. Some staff were on diets and some felt the menus were too traditional. A greater variety of menu would certainly attract some non-users of the canteen.

3 *Is the service satisfactory?*
Everybody thought it was. Canteen staff were seen as helpful and efficient. Service was quick and tables were cleared swiftly. Hygiene was good and the general atmosphere was friendly and pleasant.

4 *Is the canteen food of good quality and well-prepared?*
There were no complaints. Regular customers said the cooking was excellent. Even rare users thought the food and cooking were of a high standard.

5 *Are prices reasonable?*
Nobody rejected the canteen because of the prices. One person said the meals were "ridiculously cheap" and said she would willingly pay more to get the sort of meal she enjoyed.

Recommendations

1 The canteen should be re-decorated. Staff uniforms, crockery and table linen should match the decoration as in a smart restaurant.

2 A greater variety of menus should be offered to take account of customer preference. Perhaps regular questionnaires could be given to gain ideas on what dishes to include on the menus.

3 Canteen prices should be increased by 10% to cover the cost of the above measures. That would still leave the canteen as a cheap place to eat. If these suggestions are accepted, the canteen would certainly be improved and probably attract many more customers.

■ *Exercise 15 Recommendations for a report*

List recommendations you would make to improve TWO of the following:

a) Your local park
b) The ground of a football team you support
c) Your kitchen *or* garage
d) Your car, motorcycle *or* bicycle
e) A shop in your town

■ *Exercise 16 Reports*

Write TWO of the following reports:

a) A report on a club's activities for its annual meeting
b) A report on a car accident for the insurance company
c) A report on a new radio station for the station director
d) A report on an English examination paper for the examination board
e) A report on a package holiday for the holiday company

Some types of report are better as continuous pieces of writing. Here is a report from a newspaper on a football match. It is one person's view. It is very different from the canteen report although it still contains description and opinion.

Rovers toppled by non-league heroes

Yet again Rovers have been humiliated at home in the Cup by a non-league team. This year, it was lowly Alnwick Town of the Northern Alliance who delivered the knock-out blow.

Rovers started well. Turnbull fed his front men with a stream of intelligent passes but chance after chance was wasted. Rourke was the main culprit. Twice he skied the ball yards over the bar when it seemed easier to score.

Passes begin to go astray. By half-time, Rovers were finished. Alnwick sensed they could win. They attacked, tentatively at first, but with mounting confidence as they realised the fragile nature of their opponents' defence.

Alnwick scored with their first real shot. Gerrard, a neat, persistent striker, found himself unmarked in the box and, with cool deliberation, slid the ball under Rankin's dive.

The goal prompted some frantic but fruitless attacks by Rovers but it was no surprise to see Alnwick go further ahead. Again Gerrard found himself unmarked. This time he passed to Matthews who beat poor Rankin with a miskick.

After this second goal, Rovers' play became resigned. They were, in fact, lucky not to concede a third goal two minutes from time when Gerrard, who must have thought it was Christmas, was left unmarked again. This time Rankin palmed the shot away for a corner.

The result puts more pressure on Rovers. By the end of the game, the few fans remaining were chanting "Chalmers must go". On this form, though, no manager can save Rovers. Their cause looks lost.

This report follows the sequence of the match. There is an introduction and some comment at the end. The title is more dramatic than that of the canteen report. Newspaper readers expect a little drama. (See also pages 132–133)

■ Exercise 17 Newspaper reports

Write newspaper reports on TWO of the following:

a) A road accident
b) A visit to your town or village by a famous person
c) A demonstration or protest march
d) A court case

Essays: discussion of factual topics

On topics like

Prisons
The Care of the Elderly
Divorce
Nuclear Armaments
Unemployment

a good essay will explain *first* the hard facts, *then* people's feelings about the situation.

Planning

In your plan, as usual, list all the different points you can possibly think of on the subject. Then sort them out, under about five headings, into a sensible order.

Try *Time order:*
- how something began
- how it changed
- how it is now

or *People order:*
- the people who need something
- the people who provide it
- the people who pay for it

or *Viewpoint order:* effects on
- different age groups
- different income groups
- different religious groups
- different nationalities

or reasons *for*
reasons *against*

A combination of these often works well: for example, you could begin with Time (or "chronological") order, then go on to Viewpoint order, giving reasons for and against:

TITLE: **Nuclear Disarmament**

Time order:
- **first use** of nuclear bombs – where, when
- **effects** – huge area/ended a war (?) terrified the world
- **development** – missiles, submarines/more powerful/arms race

Reasons against:
- **control needed** – test ban treaties/spy satellites/stock piling/trust
- **protection needed** – research/alliances (NATO, SEATO)/fall-out shelters
- **effect on people** – marches, protests, apathy

Reasons for:
- **deterrent effect** – true?
- **alternatives** – "conventional" weapons (= *longer* wars, need more men and arms), wars *larger* scale now (sophisticated weapons inevitable?)

The average "O" Level essay is about 500 words – about two sides of writing in roughly five paragraphs, so *four or five main headings should be plenty*. But you must *sort out these main sections before you begin*, otherwise your essay might be full of good ideas, but be in such a jumble that they just make a bad impression. In factual essays, clear organisation is vital.

■ *Exercise 18 Essay plans and essays*

a) Write a five point plan for EACH of the following titles, arranging all the details you can think of under the five headings.

i) Democracy
ii) The equality of women
iii) Alcohol
iv) The place of religion in society

b) Using a plan you have just written, write ONE of the essays.

Facts

Find out the basic facts. Use encyclopaedias, information leaflets and newspaper articles. Look at several brief explanations and summaries, so that you get more than one set of ideas. Ask for help at libraries, a Citizens' Advice Bureau, the nearest Tourist Board office, police station or town hall. There are leaflets on a vast number of topics which affect the community and which also turn up as factual essay titles.

Opinions

Find out about people's opinions. Use newspaper articles, radio and TV programmes, which usually give you useful facts as well. One of the best ways is to discuss the topic, either in class or with friends: this means you hear several different views, and the reasons for them, and learn just how strongly people feel about their different opinions.

■ Exercise 19 Essay plans

a) Make notes on the basic facts *and also* the main opinions held on TWO of the following topics.

   The care of the elderly   Unemployment
   Divorce   Censorship

b) Using information already collected, write an essay on ONE of the two topics you prepared.

How to begin

1 One good way to begin is with *the most basic information.* Check how the dictionary defines the subject – even if you think you know what it means. Then put it in your own words *or* simply use it in quotation marks. For example, an essay on prisons could start like this:

> The dictionary defines prison like this: "Place in which person is kept in captivity, especially building to which person is legally committed, while awaiting trial or for punishment."

2 Another way is to leave this factual definition until the second paragraph and *use the first one to give the deliberately emotional story of one person's experience.* For example:

Paragraph 1

> The huge door boomed shut behind me and locked out everything normal. Daylight, traffic, the warders' voices, living noise, it all stopped. Boots echoed on stone, more doors, more echoes, my skin shivered and my stomach felt sick: boots stamped on iron stairs, wire netting caging the sides to stop a quick dive down to escape. A vile stench of disinfectant and urine, a

cell, a closed box eight by nine, walled in, muffled, buried! Oh God, this was prison.

Paragraph 2 The dictionary defines prison as a place of captivity to which men or women are "legally" committed while awaiting trial or for punishment.

Paragraph 3 The third paragraph could then be about the *other* people involved in this story – for example, here, the prisoner's victim, then his family.

Paragraph 4 The fourth paragraph could then discuss prisoners, victims and families in general.

The strength of this kind of introduction is the enormous contrast between paragraphs one and two. Get under the skin of someone who is experiencing the situation and then discuss the situation in a factual way.

3 *Follow this introduction with as accurate an explanation of the general facts as you can*: there is no room now for emotion or drama. Even when you explain very strong views which people may have on a topic, explain them calmly: describe *other* people's emotions, don't be emotional yourself.

■ *Exercise 20 Starting the essay*

a) Write the plan, then the first two paragraphs of EACH of the following essays. Make *each* opening paragraph one individual's emotional experience of the situation, followed by a paragraph defining the situation.

   i) Strikes   iii) Road Accidents
   ii) Redundancy   iv) Vivisection

b) Choose one of the titles you began working on and finish writing the essay.

Paragraphing

Separate the paragraphs very carefully, according to the main headings in your plan. Some headings may, of course, need more than one, but *the important thing is to have a strong reason for using a new paragraph*. Here is an example where a new paragraph should have been inserted:

> During the ceremony the vicar asks the bride and groom to promise, before God and before the congregation, to be faithful to each other for the rest of their lives. He talks to them of love and of "honour", or respect, for each other. That this happens in a building dedicated to God makes the promises far more serious – in fact many vicars still refuse to accept that divorce is possible, once a man and woman have made these promises, in a church wedding. The bride and groom have not only had to choose each other, they have also had to choose new clothes, a honeymoon hotel and a place to live together when the honeymoon is over, all of which cost a lot of money.

Of course there was a change of topic – *and* a change of mood from solemn to down-to-earth – in line 8 after "church wedding", so continuing the same paragraph was an obvious mistake.

Variety

Stop an essay from getting dull by changing its mood. You include different *ideas* in the subject-matter, so include different moods.

■ Exercise 21 Essay plans

a) Write a plan for THREE of the following essays. In each plan include five main headings, detailed points under each one, and mark with an asterisk the points which might be used to make the mood of the essays less serious.

Modern marriage	Modern architecture
Soccer hooliganism	The Welfare State

b) Using a plan you have just worked on, write one of the essays.

Ending the essay

There has to be a clear conclusion and it should usually take several lines. In a narrative essay you might want to end with something unexpected and therefore use a paragraph of two or three lines. In a factual essay a short "surprise ending" is much less likely. Instead, *sum up the main points already made, ending with a reference to what is likely to be the next development.* Do this briefly for two reasons:

i) to show that you are deliberately summing up, repeating ideas to emphasise them and end the essay in a strong, sensible way;

ii) to avoid making the repetition seem messy, unnecessary and boring.

■ Exercise 22 Factual essays

Write the plan, then the essay, on ONE of the following topics:

a) The extinction of wild life   d) Pollution

b) The consumer society   e) Crime

c) Superstition   f) Poverty

Include: i) five main headings in the plan

           ii) more than one viewpoint

           iii) a change of mood in one of the paragraphs

(Allow yourself an hour to write 500 words.)

4 Words

Technical terms

Technical terms are words and phrases connected with particular activities. In a garage, you would hear:

crankshaft	differential	gasket
sparking plug	manifold	timing
carburettor	bush	grease gun

Those are some of the technical terms of motor mechanics.

■ *Exercise 23 Technical terms*

Make a list of at least *eight* technical terms used in ONE of the following:

a) Cooking *or* woodwork
b) Computers
c) Football *or* cricket *or* hockey *or* tennis
d) Popular music
e) Gardening *or* photography *or* painting

Use technical terms freely in writing if your readers are as expert as you. If they are not, be careful. The ordinary motorist probably knows:

accelerator	clutch	indicator

but may not understand:

manifold	bush	differential

Sometimes you need to use an unfamiliar technical term. In that case, you should explain the meaning **simply**. If you use the word "aorta" while describing the blood system, do not define it as:

the great trunk of the arterial system issuing from the left ventricle.

Your reader will be more confused. A better definition would be:

a large tube in the body carrying blood from the heart.

■ *Exercise 24 Simple explanations of technical terms*

Explain THREE of the following terms in simple language.

a) "Poach", as used in cooking.
b) "Differential", as used in car mechanics.
c) "Decrease", as used in knitting.
d) "Sweeper", as used in football.
e) "Isobar", as used in weather forecasting.
f) "Prune", as used in gardening.
g) "Perforation", as used in stamp collecting.
h) "Ground bait", as used in fishing.

Jargon

Language which is so full of specialist words that it baffles an ordinary reader is called "jargon". It is not clever to make a reader feel like that. You may have been annoyed yourself at some time because a form or paper was impossible to understand. Never annoy *your* readers in that way.

■ *Exercise 25 Explaining "specialist" words*

These sentences have "specialist" words in bold type. Look up those words in a good dictionary and re-write the sentences so a non-specialist could understand them:

a) The archaeologist **excavated** several **shards** from the site.
b) The school had a **pedagogical** approach that was **heuristic**.
c) During the experiment, **combustion** took place in the **retort**.
d) The constable **apprehended** the man while he was committing a **felony**.
e) She **adjourned** the meeting because there was not a **quorum**.
f) He **marinated** the meat and prepared the **legumes**.
g) The optician was not sure if. Bob had **myopia** or **hypermetropia**.
h) Although **par** for the hole was three, Susan managed an **eagle**.
i) He broke his right **patella** and left **tibia** in the accident.
j) It was an **isosceles** triangle with **vertices** A, B and C.

Officialese

A type of jargon frequently met is "officialese", the language too often used in official documents. Writers of "officialese" like to use *ten* long, difficult words where *one* short, easy word would do. In "officialese" people will be:

temporary units of population.

Never write "officialese" yourself. You may let a character in your writing use it to show that person is pompous or stupid. But, remember, "officialese" is *bad* English.

■ *Exercise 26 Re-writing "officialese"*

Put these "officialese" sentences into clear, direct English:

a) There is a considerable and developing probability that the climatic conditions will deteriorate rapidly.

b) In view of our present deficiencies related to cash-flow, it is now necessary to take advantage of your loan facilities.

c) A confident estimate of two hundred habitation units should be added to the operational housing register in the ongoing construction phase.

d) At this moment in time, my employment potential is not being realised in the context of an appropriate position.

e) We are in the process of investigating the implementation of some corrective initiative aimed at rectifying the situation.

f) The proposed swimming facility is likely to be detrimental to the visual amenity of the local neighbourhood.

g) Linguistic development in the initial period of infant life is enhanced by the practice of oral communication.

h) This notice formally excludes all personnel from entry to this area.

There are three rules to keep if you want to avoid "jargon" and "officialese".

1 **Do not use words that are not needed.**
2 **Use familiar words.**
3 **Use precise words.**

5 Spelling: "e" – using it and losing it

The letter "e" is often silent in English words but, even though it is silent, it can change the sound of a preceding vowel if there is just one consonant between them. Look at these two lists:

tap	tape
them	theme
rid	ride
cub	cube
rod	rode

The vowels in the right-hand column have different sounds from those in the left-hand column because the letter "e" has been added.

■ Exercise 27 The silent "e"

Fill in the gaps in each sentence using the words in brackets:

a) George stole the _____ of beans so he got the _____. (can, cane)
b) Fancy using sticky _____ to mend a broken _____. (tap, tape)
c) The gorilla gave the _____ lady a _____. (hug, huge)
d) The lecturer explained the _____ of the novel to _____. (them, theme)
e) The mechanic was in a _____ because he had lost his oily _____. (rag, rage)
f) I took a _____ to the butcher to get some _____. (trip, tripe)
g) He said he had not had a _____ for a week so I _____ him. (bit, bite)
h) The elephant decided to _____ down on the building _____. (sit, site)
i) Helen fixed the notice to a _____ tree with a _____. (pin, pine)
j) Try and _____ the bottle of _____. (win, wine)

An "e" can change the sound of a preceding vowel, even if it is not at the end of a word. Here are some examples with both the "e" and the vowel it changes in bold type.

later   meter   invited   cones   used

Notice that in some of these words the "e" stops being silent and makes a sound. Many English words are formed by adding endings to other words. A word like "book" can be used to create a whole range of words:

book + **able**=bookable   book + **ing** = booking
book + **ish** = bookish   book + **let** = booklet

When words with a final "e" are treated in this way, it is sometimes difficult to know whether to keep the "e" or lose it. The general rule is:

When an ending is added to a word ending in "e", the "e" is dropped before a vowel but kept before a consonant.

so:

hope + ing becomes hoping **and loses the "e"**,
hope + less becomes hopeless **and keeps the "e"**.

■ *Exercise 28   Keeping the "e" or losing it?*

Add the endings given to each word. Does the final "e" stay or go?

a) time   *add*   -ly, -ing, -less.
b) cube   *add*   -ism, ic, -oid.
c) home   *add*   -ing, -stead, -ed.
d) late   *add*   -er, -ness, -ly.
e) note   *add*   -able, -worthy, -let.

Like most spelling rules, the one given above has exceptions. Many of these are covered by another rule:

The final "e" is kept even before a vowel if it is needed:
either to show that a preceding "g" or "c" keeps its soft sound
or to show that the word is a different one from another spelt the same.

So: change + **ing** = changing
the "e" is dropped because the "i" after the "g" keeps it soft,
but: change + **able** = changeable
the "e" is kept because, without it, "g" would become a hard sound.

Also: singe + **ing**   singeing
the "e" is needed, not to keep the "g" soft, but to stop confusion
with sing + **ing** (= singing)
There are words, however, that do not follow these rules. Try to
remember the following normally accepted spellings:

mile + **age** = mileage
rate + **able** = rateable
age + **ing** = ageing

■ *Exercise 29 Correcting mis-spellings*

Correct the spelling in these sentences:

a) My favourite pop star was wearing holy socks.
b The government made swinging cuts in expenditure.
c) You are too close to the fire because I can smell your hair
singing.
d) What is the milage from here to Leicester.
e) The ratable value of my house has increased.
f) There is a storm rageing in the English Channel.
g) Will you please stop changeing your mind?
h) She is the only daughter of aging parents.
i) Have you seen the racing on television?
j) The weather is very changable for August.

6 Exercises for revision

■ Exercise 30 Instructions

Write instructions for your neighbour who will look after your house, cat and house plants while you are away for two weeks in December. She will have a key.

■ Exercise 31 Instructions

Write clear, simple instructions in 150 words on ONE of the following:

a) Developing a camera film
b) Cooking a Christmas dinner
c) Bathing a baby
d) Topping up with petrol, oil and water at a self-service garage
e) Evacuating a large building during a fire alarm

■ Exercise 32 Job descriptions

Write a description of the job of ONE of the following:

a) A children's nurse
b) A bus driver
c) A park attendant
d) A librarian
e) A secretary

■ Exercise 33 Newspaper advertisements

Write newspaper advertisements for TWO of the following:
a) A new restaurant about to open
b) A 7-day package holiday abroad
c) A double bill at the cinema or A play at the theatre
d) A pop concert or A piano recital
e) A large new sports centre

■ Exercise 34 Accident report

Your car or bike has been in an accident at a roundabout. Using 150–200 words, describe accurately what happened for an insurance company.

■ *Exercise 35 Game description*

Describe any game in about 250 words; mention equipment, rules and scoring.

■ *Exercise 36 Description*

Describe the street where you live in about 250 words for a pen-friend.

■ *Exercise 37 Confused sentences*

Re-write the following sentences so they have clear meanings:

a) Ian handed the old man his blue velvet jacket.
b) She decided not to wear her summer dress because it was wet.
c) When and where did you say you felt the pain?
d) Emma was surprised to see Aunt Jane on her moped.
e) I hate cocoa when it is hot but when it is cold I drink gallons of it.
f) Mrs Green told her mother about Jane and she gave a big smile.
g) The stone statue crashed on the chair and smashed its legs.
h) Mr and Mrs Wright let Helen and Tom see the kittens before they ate.

■ *Exercise 38 Word order causing confusion*

Re-write the following sentences so the meanings are clear:

a) That is the hospital near the football ground where I was born.
b) The butcher wrapped up the sheep's head with a big smile.
c) I saw a pillar box walking down the street.
d) You'll attract flies wearing yellow trousers.
e) The captain saw the girls running through his old telescope.
f) The plumber mended the tap on the bath that was leaking.
g) Hanging from the ceiling, Melanie noticed a long, dusty cobweb.
h) He gave the cat a herring wearing a blue suit.

■ *Exercise 39 Dashes or brackets?*

Put dashes or brackets where needed in the following sentences:

a) He looked at the "weapon" a broom handle with a grim smile.
b) They Hurst and Peters scored England's goals in the 1966 final.
c) My guide was called Pedro Spanish for Peter.
d) Shantung a soft Chinese silk was used to make the ceremonial robes.
e) I refused his offer £500 in used notes and left the room.
f) The car a 1903 Darraq was rescued from a cowshed in Clitheroe.
g) Your order the one for 500 left-handed chisels has gone to York.
h) He is suffering from diarrhoea note the spelling.

■ *Exercise 40 Memoranda*

Write a memorandum on ONE of the following topics. Use the recommended layout:

a) Informing all staff that, in future, they will be paid monthly.
b) Telling section heads about a new staff discount on company products.
c) Commenting on punctuality.
d) Asking the transport section to provide two cars on a certain day.
e) Inviting comment on new office or factory lighting.

■ *Exercise 41 Memorandum*

Write a memorandum responding to one of those listed in Exercise 40.

■ *Exercise 42 Reports*

Write ONE of the following reports:

a) A report on the central heating system for a potential buyer
b) A report on a new cosmetic for a consumer research organisation
c) A report on a cheap ball pen for an office manager
d) A report on English weather in July for a visitor from abroad

■ Exercise 43 Newspaper report

Write a newspaper report on ONE of the following:

a) A local election
b) A bank robbery
c) The tragic death of a well-known local personality
d) A charity disco
e) A sports event

■ Exercise 44 Essay plans

a) Write a six point plan for EACH of the following titles.
b) List all the details you think of, under these main points.
c) Mark with an asterisk the points you could use to lighten the mood.

Man is the weakest of all animals
The importance of colour
Travel broadens the mind
Money is the root of all evil
World poverty

■ Exercise 45 Factual essay

Write ONE of the essays listed in Exercise 44.

■ Exercise 46 Finding information + factual essay

a) Make notes on the basic facts *and also* the main opinions held on TWO of the following.

Censorship   Advertising
Drunken driving   Vandalism
Trades Unions   The monarchy in Britain

b) Write *both* of the essays which you have prepared notes on.

■ Exercise 47 Technical words

Explain TWO of the following words in simple language:

a) "pointing", as used in building
b) "foundation", as used in cosmetics
c) "fuse", as used in electrical appliances
d) "trump", as used in card games
e) "depression", as used in weather forecasting
f) "headline", as used in newspapers

■ Exercise 48 Re-writing "officialese"

Put the following sentences into clear simple English:

a) Please adjust the illumination sources within this living space to facilitate maximum vision.
b) Expedite the despatch of fuel suitable for oil-fired domestic heating.
c) Anybody apprehended unlawfully removing merchandise will be prosecuted forthwith.
d) The time-scale allocated for this particular assignment has proved inadequate for the demands involved in its execution.
e) All male and female persons over the adult qualifying age and engaged in gainful employment will be liable.
f) Buildings associated with agricultural activity will be subject to a tax that will be calculated at the appropriate level.
g) It is difficult at this particular juncture to suggest any positive solution to the problem as presented.
h) In the event that the threatened rail strike becomes an actuality, road transport should be utilised for the despatch of merchandise.

■ *Exercise 49 The silent "e"*

Fill in the gaps in the following sentences using the words in brackets:

a) We _____ he does not catch us on the _____ again. (hop, hope)

b) The lawyer issued a _____ before I could _____ to explain. (writ, write)

c) The dog _____ his tail when he sees Dad's _____. (wags, wages)

d) The lion _____ like their food cut into _____. (cubs, cubes)

e) As he came down the _____, he started to _____ his tea. (slop, slope)

f) Do not _____ at everyone who comes through the _____ in the hedge. (gap, gape)

g) Every time Clive eats a pomegranate, he gets a _____ in his _____. (pip, pipe)

h) The _____ did _____ arrive. (not, note)

■ *Exercise 50 Keeping the "e" or losing it*

Add the endings given to each of these words. Does the final "e" stay or go?

a) change   *add*   -ling, -able, -ing
b) mile   *add*   -age, -stone
c) age   *add*   -ed, -ing, -less
d) singe   *add*   -ing, -ed
e) hole   *add*   -ing, -y
f) rate   *add*   -ing, -able
g) ice   *add*   -icle, -ing, -y
h) wave   *add*   -ing, -let, -y

Sample examination paper

There are many examination boards throughout the country and the examinations they set are quite different. You should get sample papers of the examination you will take. Regular timed practice with these will certainly improve your chances. Make sure that the papers are recent. Changes in style do occur and if the papers you are working with are ten years old, you could have a nasty surprise in the examination hall.

Clearly it is not possible to include samples of all examination types in this book. The papers given, however, are typical and they certainly test the same skills as the examination you will take. It would be useful for you to attempt them in the time allowed.

August Examination 1984 – Ordinary Level

ENGLISH LANGUAGE – Syllabus 1

Paper 1

Wednesday, 6th August, 9.30 am to 11.00 am
1 hour and 30 minutes allowed
Answer both questions
The use of dictionaries in this examination is prohibited.

1 Choose ONE of the following for composition. About *one hour* should be spent on this question.   (35 marks)

a) The advantages and disadvantages of always saying exactly what you think.

b) "We have been led to believe that scientists can solve all our problems. They actually cause more problems than they solve." What do you feel about this opinion?

c) Mountains.

d) "O to be in England now that April's here." Do you share this view of April in England?

e) "School days are the happiest days." Does your experience tend to make you agree or disagree with this statement?

f) Write a story in which an overheard remark causes trouble.

g) Do you think holidays abroad are more fun than holidays in England?

2 Answer ONE of the following. About *half an hour* should be spent on this question.   (15 marks)

a) You have a part-time job at a playgroup *or* as a weekend assistant in a shop *or* as a newspaper boy or girl (*or* as a petrol pump attendant). A substitute takes over because you are on holiday. Write clear instructions for your substitute.

b) You have recently written to a mail order firm, complaining that a garment sent to you had been found on receipt to be torn and of the wrong size. You have asked for a replacement. After more than three weeks, you have received no reply. Write a second letter of complaint.

c) You read a letter in your local newspaper complaining about the selfish attitude of modern young people. Write a letter to the editor supporting or attacking this view.

d) Write a confidential reference for a friend who has applied for *one* of the following jobs:
   i) Motor mechanic in a large garage
   ii) Nurse in an old people's home
   iii) Assistant keeper in a zoo
   iv) Receptionist in an expensive hotel

August Examination, 1984 – Ordinary Level
ENGLISH LANGUAGE – Syllabus 1

Paper 2

Wednesday, 6th August, 2.00 pm to 3.45 pm
1 hour and 45 minutes allowed

Answer Questions 1 *and* 2, *one* section from Question 3 and *one* section from Question 4.

The use of dictionaries in this examination is prohibited.

1 Write a summary of the following passage in good, continuous prose, using not more than 120 words. State at the end of the summary the number of words you have used. The passage contains 360 words.   (16 marks)

The effects of air pollution may not be dramatic but some of the unpleasant substances now released into our atmosphere can cause a gradual poisoning of the human frame. This slowly but surely reduces the quality of life for those who are vulnerable. Respiratory diseases such as bronchitis which cause the loss of countless working days each year are made much worse by regular exposure to a polluted atmosphere. In areas where there is heavy industry, clothes get dirty quicker and this produces a faster rate of deterioration. Sulphuric acid, a common pollutant, can cause tights to ladder and it is obvious to all how the paintwork on buildings is affected. Perhaps less obvious is the corrosion which air pollution brings about in metal and brickwork. Many of the most beautiful old buildings in Europe are being destroyed in this way and where governments act to preserve these monuments of the past, the costs are often high. Air pollution is expensive.

Air pollution also affects plants and this is vital because plants are an important link in the chain of life. They take in carbon dioxide from the atmosphere and give off oxygen. Air pollution can reduce this capacity and also slows down growth. It has been estimated that agriculture loses millions of pounds each year because of the reduced crop yield brought about by air pollution. In some parts of Britain there is an annual deposit of 125 tons of polluting material per square mile. This deposit contains many substances which are deadly to plants such as ammonia and chlorine.

Animals, of course, get their food either directly or indirectly from plants. They will be affected by any event which destroys plant life but air pollution can also affect them directly. Depending on the particular pollutant present, animals can suffer from heart disease, breathing problems or even arthritis. The central nervous system of men and animals is sensitive to minor changes in the air breathed.

It is sometimes claimed that it would cost more to prevent air pollution that to endure its effects. This is short sighted. Air pollution threatens us and our environment. We cannot afford to ignore it.

2 Read the following passage carefully and then answer the questions on it. (20 marks)

The first reaction of young visitors to the Zoo to the elephant is of the "gee-whiz" variety, and is due mainly to its size. Although scientists very properly point out that the animal possesses other features at least
5 equally remarkable, it would be difficult to argue with the conventional point of view. The attraction of sheer bulk is irresistible, and no excuse is therefore necessary for beginning an account of the elephant body with this most conspicuous of its many inter-
10 esting features.

A large African bull may stand 3.5 metres at the shoulder and weigh 7 tonnes. It is thus the largest living land animal. Only the giraffe exceeds the elephant in height, and only the hippopotamus and
15 white rhinoceros are even remotely comparable in weight. But the superior height of the giraffe, which may exceed 5.5 metres, is due mainly to the length of its neck and legs, and no existing hippopotamus or

rhinoceros has been known to weigh more than 4
20 tonnes. To find animals that greatly exceed the
elephant in bulk it is necessary to go to some extinct
reptiles and mammals, and to the living whales. For
example, the dinosaur Brachiosaurus had a weight of
50 tonnes, and an extinct relation of the rhinoceros,
25 known as Baluchitherium, was about the size of a
double-decker bus. The living blue whale, with a
weight of between 120 and 150 tonnes, is larger still,
its bulk exceeding that of twenty full grown African
elephants. It is, in fact, the largest animal that has ever
30 lived on earth.

There is a belief among hunters that the height of
an elephant at the shoulder is equivalent to twice the
circumference of the foot. This is a rough and ready
guide, but does not hold good for young, growing
35 animals, when it gives too high a figure. The size of
a domesticated elephant is usually assessed by
throwing a measure over the shoulders, bringing the
ends to the ground, subtracting 40 centimetres to
allow for the curvature of the back, and dividing the
40 result by two. But this again is a very unreliable
method owing to the variations in back curvature in
animals of different ages, and the old, good guide is
a wall scale with a moving slide that can be brought
down horizontally until the elephant can just stand
45 under it.

Likewise, for measuring weight, there is no alternative but to persuade the animal to stand on a weight-
bridge. Faulty measurements and wild guesses at
tonnage are responsible for many exaggerated esti-
50 mates of the size of the elephant's body, and such
statistics, especially where wild elephants are
concerned, should always be regarded with the
deepest suspicion.

Richard Carrington

a) Choose FOUR of the following words. For each
word chosen give another word or short phrases

which could replace it in the passage without changing the meaning.

irresistible (line 7)
exceeds (line 13)
existing (line 18)
equivalent (line 32)
assessed (line 36)
exaggerated (line 49) (4 marks)

b) Why does the author give "no excuse" for beginning with the size of the elephants? (2 marks)

c) The giraffe is much taller than the elephant but considerably lighter. Why is this? (4 marks)

d) Explain in your own words *one* way of estimating the elephant's height and why it is unreliable. (4 marks)

e) Explain the meaning of the following expressions as they are used in the passage:
   i) "most conspicuous of its many interesting features" (lines 9–10)
   ii) "an extinct relation of the rhinoceros" (line 24)
                                              (3 marks)

f) Why might stories about the size of wild elephants be untrue? (3 marks)

3 Answer *either* section (a) *or* section (b). (8 marks)

a) Re-write the following passage in paragraphs, inserting punctuation and capital letters.

david put down the radio times and turned on the tv he flopped into the armchair it was eight oclock time for his favourite comedy programme he had been watching only ten minutes when the bell rang bother muttered david but he went to open the door it was aunt mildred hello auntie said david without enthusiasm do come in no i wont just now she replied ive just come to get uncle berts present i asked you to collect in town david clapped a hand to his forehead in dismay i forgot he exclaimed.

b) Re-write the following passage in not more than *five* sentences without using *and* or *but* or *so*. You may re-arrange the information but you must not omit any.

Charles Dickens was a writer. Many people think he was the greatest English novelist. His childhood was unhappy. His father was often in prison for debt. At the age of twelve Dickens was sent to work in a blacking factory. Later he became a reporter. He started writing serial stories for magazines. His work was immediately popular. Readers enjoyed his humour. They loved his strange and wonderful characters. Dickens was a stern critic of Victorian society. He was especially concerned with the plight of children. This is shown in books like *Oliver Twist*.

4 Answer *either* Section (a) or Section (b)   (6 marks)

a) Choose TWO of the following groups of words. Compose a sentence for each word in these two groups, to show that you *clearly* understand the difference in meanings. Write six sentences in all:

i) stolid	unruffled	heartless
ii) possible	likely	promising
iii) strayed	straggled	scattered

b) Choose THREE of the following words, and for each write two sentences to show clearly
  i) the literal meaning and
  ii) the metaphorical usage, as in the example.
     Write six sentences in all.
  Example: *riveted*
  i) The metal plate was *riveted* to the wing of the car. (literal)
  ii) His eyes were *riveted* to the television screen. (metaphorical)

  crusty   spin   stormy   torn   velvet

Another way of using this book

You can use this Contents list for revision or just to work on a particular problem.

230 ANOTHER WAY OF USING THIS BOOK

Unit	Contents	pages	Exercises	(pages)
	Words			
4	Using the right words	120	22–5	(120–1)
2	Learning new words	62	13–16, 25–8	(62–3, 71–2)
3	Saying it briefly	89	13–16, 23–4	(89–91, 97)
5	Saying it more powerfully	142	15–21, 27–8	(143–6, 149)
6	Common mistakes	173	10–15, 22	(175–7, 184)
7	Technical terms	207	23–4, 47	(207–8, 217)
	Jargon	208	26	(208)
	Officialese	209	27, 48	(209, 217)
	Spelling			
1	Words ending – 1	34	35	(38)
2	Double letters	64	17, 18, 29	(64–5, 72)
3	Making words plural	92	17, 25	(93, 97)
4	-sc- and -cc-	122	26, 37	(122, 126)
5	-i before -e (and exceptions)	147	22, 29	(147, 150)
7	'e' using it and losing it	210	27–9, 49–50	(210–12, 218)
6	Words often confused	178	16, 17, 23	(178–9, 185)
3	'have' not 'of'	82		

Answers to multiple choice comprehension questions

Exercise 1 (*page 152*) **B**
Exercise 2 (*page 181*) **1D 2D 3B 4A 5D 6E**

Acknowledgements

We are grateful to the following for permission to reproduce copyright material:

George Allen & Unwin Ltd for an adapted extract from *The Body* by A. Smith; author's Agents and the Estate of H. E. Bates for an extract from his *The Vanished World* pub. Michael Joseph Ltd; Wm. Collins plc for an extract from *The Decline of an English Village* by R. Page, previously published by Davis Poynter Ltd; author's agents for an extract from *Brighton Rock* by Graham Greene, pub. Wm. Heinemann Ltd & The Bodley Head Ltd; author's agents and the Estate of Mrs. Frieda Lawrence Ravagli for an extract from *The Rainbow* by D. H. Lawrence; Oxford University Press for an adapted extract from the Introduction to *Children's Games in Street and Playground* (1969) by Iona & Peter Opie; University of London School Examinations Department for a specimen answer sheet.

We have been unable to trace the copyright owner of an extract from *The Sunday Times* (1983) and would appreciate any information which would enable us to do so.

Y047981

Contem... ... in
Alaska ... ... he
can fr... ... n.
Thankfully, her laptop travels with her and she has written
... way through all fifty states and over fifty countries.

Lizzie has been honored to win the Golden Heart Award and
HOLT Medallion, and has been named a finalist three times
for Romance Writers of America's prestigious RITA Award®,
but her main claim to fame is that she lost on *Jeopardy!*

For more about Lizzie and her books, please visit
www.lizzieshane.com.

Praise for Lizzie Shane:

'The endearing characters will capture readers' hearts from the
first page ... It's hard not to fall in love with this spirited tale'
Publishers Weekly

'*Once Upon a Puppy* is a must read for all fans of rom-coms
and contemporary romance ... I enjoyed this sweet
heartfelt rivalry more than I can put into words'
Urban Book Reviews

'An irresistible blend of heart, humour, nostalgic moments,
misunderstandings, family, friendship, tension, chemistry,
attraction, spirited shenanigans, Christmas cheer, and a
whole lot of puppy love' *What's Better Than Books?*

'A dog lovers dream come true, mixed in with Christmas and
the most adorable romance' *Breakfast at Shelby's*

'A magical read ... If you read one holiday romance this year
make it this one, I don't think you'll regret it!' *Novel Gossip*

'Could not put it down ... Beautifully written'
Harlequin Junkie

'Shane's heart-warming plot, perfect mix of small-town
charm and buoyant wit, perfectly imperfect human characters,
and adorable canines truly capture the thrill of love and the
magic of the dogs-and-people connection' *Booklist*

By Lizzie Shane

The Twelve Dogs of Christmas
Once Upon a Puppy
To All the Dogs I've Loved Before